# Country Anecdotes

# Country Anecdotes

Chosen by
HUMPHREY PHELPS

ROBERT HALE · LONDON

© *Humphrey Phelps 1990*
*First published in Great Britain 1990*

Robert Hale Limited
Clerkenwell House
Clerkenwell Green
London EC1R 0HT

**British Library Cataloguing in Publication Data**

Country anecdotes.
1. Anecdotes in English. Special subjects. Countryside –
Anthologies
I. Phelps, Humphrey
828′.02

ISBN 0–7090–4022–9

Set in Ehrhardt by
Derek Doyle & Associates, Mold, Clwyd.
Printed in Great Britain by
St Edmundsbury Press, Bury St Edmunds, Suffolk.
Bound by WBC Bookbinders Limited.

# Contents

To Brian Stevens,
who thought of the
idea

# Introduction

Opinions differ about what is or is not an anecdote. My dictionary's interpretation is 'a detached incident, unpublished details of history'. Nearly all the pieces in this collection have been detached from published works, several of them contain more than one incident, and a few may be regarded as details of social history.

This anthology presents one person's choice of anecdotes, based upon my own definition of the word. An incident or a series of incidents, which make a short story, a small item of information or interest; the reader will discover that I have interpreted the term very loosely. I have eschewed the popular notion that an anecdote must necessarily be amusing and brief. Some of the pieces are short, some are a thousand words or more in length. Some are comic, others are tragic, pensive, sublime or ridiculous, strange, informative or descriptive, while still others fit into none of these categories. The only thing they have in common is that they all have a rural setting. Although I trust that they tell a story or make some point; all anecdotes must, I think, have a point and that point should be reasonably sharp. Several show the point of the spontaneous wit, the humour and the sagacity of the countryman, which were more in evidence in the past than they are today. These anecdotes illustrate many aspects of country life and work. I should like to have been able to furnish examples of most aspects, but that would have been an impossible task. Country life and work are too varied and cast to encompass within the bounds of one book, even if I had had the ability to do so.

An anthology should contain both the familiar and the unfamiliar extract. Not too many of the former, but just enough to make the reader feel at home. Ardent readers of country books may find too many familiar stories or even wonder why some of their favourite rural anecdotes are not included. But that is a risk shared by both readers and compilers of anthologies. I can only hope that that risk is largely avoided here and that readers will find the familiar anecdotes they want to find and not too many of the ones they don't want. Much more, I hope they will find many which are new to them and that these will lead them to the books from which the anecdotes came. If this should be the case, this anthology will have performed the proper purpose of an anthology: namely, to supply present interest and lead the way to future and extended interest and pleasure. I have included interest as well as pleasure because, although some of these anecdotes are amusing, some are by no means pleasant. They illustrate the grim lives and conditions endured by country people in the past, poverty and hardship, and one heart-rending story of the little boy transported for life.

In my choice of anecdotes I have been guided by three simple rules. One, every anecdote should be factual. Two, to include only anecdotes of the English countryside. Three, to offer only anecdotes from the eighteenth, nineteenth and twentieth centuries.

From the beginning I was convinced that rule one was essential and must be observed faithfully if this collection was to have any validity. It has meant the loss of many excellent anecdotes which in all probability are perfectly true. I have in mind those which are to be found in books which are autobiographical in tone but cast in a fictional mould. Such books as *Memoirs of a Foxhunting Man* by Siegfried Sassoon, *Corduroy, Silver Ley* and *The Cherry Tree* by Adrian Bell, *Portrait of Elmbury* by John Moore, and *Lark Rise to Candleford* by Flora Thompson.

Other anecdotes in quite a number of books presented as factual were rejected because on close examination I did not think they had the ring of sound truth. There was also difficulty with many others, especially some of the short, humorous ones, in that such stories have often been improved on or embroidered in the telling. Most of these were also rejected, while others which seemed to me to possess veracity have been retained.

Rule two was dictated for two reasons: because my knowledge of country literature other than English is limited and because a more ambitious project, covering the whole of the British Isles, would also have made this book far too large. Size — and weight too – is an important factor in a book of this sort. If it is too large and heavy, it is not an ideal bedside book; for surely an anthology should be designed for reading in bed. I confess that more than once I was tempted to break this rule. For instance, England, oddly enough, seemed to have a dearth of suitable, recorded anecdotes of country children and village schools, yet *Schoolin's Log* by Llewellyn Jones had several splendid ones of children and school in remote North Pembrokeshire. The Cotswolds and East Anglia, especially East Anglia, provided a plenitude of splendid stories. Many, alas, had to be cast aside or this book would have become a collection of only Cotswold and East Anglian anecdotes. On the other hand, some regions, and particularly the North, supplied surprisingly few. I am quite willing to admit that this imbalance may have been caused by my deficiency, but not altogether, as many northern country books are fiction.

Female writers too, are not well represented, and again I think for the same reason. Such writers as Doreen Wallace, Winifred Holtby, Mary Webb, Constance Holme and Sheila Kaye-Smith have concentrated upon writing fiction. If these ladies had chosen to cast their material in factual form, the balance here between the regions as well as the balance between the sexes would have been more even. However, balance in either of these senses was not my objective. Some country writers, male and female, many of them very well known, have not provided me with the type of stories I wanted. In the context of a book, the incidents were fine, but once removed many were just not strong enough to stand on their own. Other writers provided few anecdotes, good or bad. Before I began deliberately to look for anecdotes, I had supposed that the works of Richard Jefferies would be a rich source but it proved otherwise.

Some attempt has been made to group the stories thematically, although this was not always easy. Many pieces contain a combination of subjects; others, although the subject matter differed, formed natural pairs or groups, but each section has some thematic unity, except the last but one, where stories which defied any classification are conveniently brought together.

Several of the anecdotes have been extracted from books of memoirs, and many of the incidents recorded occurred long before the publication of the books.

Clergymen, especially of the Church of England, by their words or deeds, have been a fruitful source. Often their deeds were eccentric, but eccentricity is not confined to parsons or to humans in general. Animals, which on the whole are more rational, can also behave eccentrically, as can the weather. Eccentricity makes frequent appearances because it is one of the best ingredients for a good story. Strange occurrences or experiences have a section, although many of them could have fitted into some other section.

Included are a number of incidents relating to the Tithe War, so perhaps a note of explanation is appropriate. In medieval times one tenth of 'annual increase' of farm produce became the legal tithe payment. From 1704 until the Tithe Act of 1936 the Church authorities collected the tithes through a branch of the corporation known as Queen Anne's Bounty. After various changes in the nineteenth century, tithes were re-organized in 1925. The tithes were then levelled on a basis in line with the high prices of the post-war years. As the value of farm land and produce fell, discontentment about tithes increased, which led to the Tithe War of the 1930s. Owing to the slump in the prices of corn, arable counties, particularly in East Anglia, suffered badly from the tithes. And so did Kent, where the tithe rates were particularly high. The vexed question was investigated by a Royal Commission, and in 1936 new legislation provided for the end of the tithe charge from 1996. The Government paid the Church £53 million and lay tithe-owners £17 million in compensation but with the intention of recovering the money from farmers over a sixty-year period, with the power to raid the bank account or seize the milk cheque of any farmer who defaulted on his annual payments. However, in 1987 tithes were suspended because the cost of gathering them had become too great. At last the tithe-protesters had won the war.

This collection presents only a sample of country anecdotes. A rich vein has, of necessity, been virtually untapped. Almost every countryman must have had a store of anecdotes, most of which have never been recorded and which if not already lost, will soon be lost forever.

'I remember when ...': these words were the precursor to many an anecdote, in field, market-place or inn in the days when everyone in a country parish knew everyone else and when several men worked together in the fields and could talk without being deafened by the noise of machinery, while forking sheaves or hay, hoeing roots by hand, and so forth. The work was hard and the hours were long but the labour was lightened by the rhythm of the work, and men could talk and joke as they worked. Soon hardly anyone will remember forking sheaves or hay, working in the fields day after day in company, or the stories which helped to lighten the labour and the hours. As long as life and speech remain, there will be anecdotes, but I do not think country anecdotes of the future will be as plentiful, as rich or as varied as they have been.

# Acknowledgements

My grateful thanks are due to those authors, publishers and other copyright owners who have allowed me to use copyright material. Reproduction is by permission of the publisher unless otherwise stated.

E.L.A: 'The Oak Gives up its Secret' (October 1935) by permission of the editor of *The Countryman*

Margery Allingham: '*The Oaken Heart*' (Michael Joseph, 1941), by permission of Curtis Brown

Fred Archer: two extracts from *The Distant Scene* (Hodder & Stoughton, 1967) by permission of the author

H.E. Bates: *Country Life* (Penguin, 1943) by permission of Laurence Pollinger Ltd and the estate of H.E. Bates

F.W. Baty: two extracts from *The Forest of Dean* (Robert Hale, 1952) by permission of the author

Lillian Beckwith: two extracts from *About My Father's Business* (Hutchinson, 1971)

Adrian Bell: five extracts from *My Own Master* (Faber, 1961) by permission of Mrs Marjorie Bell

S.L. Bensusan: two extracts from *Back of Beyond* (Blandford, 1945)

Justin and Edith Brooke: four extracts from *Suffolk Prospect* (Faber, 1963)

Mavis Budd: two extracts from *Fit For a Duchess* (Dent, 1970) by permission of Aitken & Stone Ltd

Raymond Bush: *Fruit Salad* (Cassell, 1947) by permission of Laurence Pollinger Ltd and the estate of Raymond Bush

John Byng: *The Torrington Diaries* (Eyre & Spottiswoode, 1954)

Henry J. Carr: 'The Fox Diviner', by permission of the editor of *The Field*

Leonard Clark: *A Fool in the Forest* (Dobson, 1965)

John Stewart Collis: two extracts from *While Following the Plough* (Cape, 1946) by permission of A.P. Watt Ltd, on behalf of Michael Holroyd

R.W. Corbett: 'Cormorant and Herons', (Field Bedside Book, Robson, 1984) by permission of the editor of *The Field*

*The Countryman:* 'It Don't Matter'(1935), 'A Very Great Storm' (1945), by permisison of the editor of *The Countryman*

*The Countryman Book* (Odhams, 1948): 'Not So Deficient', by permission of the editor of *The Countryman*

George Ewart Evans: *Ask the Fellows who Cut the Hay* (Faber, 2nd edition, 1961) *Spoken History* (Faber, 1984)

P. Fforde: 'Poaching by Candlelight', *(The Countryman Anthology, 1962)* by permission of the editor of *The Countryman*

Sir Newman Flower: 'Walks with Thomas Hardy' (1945) by permission of the editor of *The Countryman*

Colin Fraser: *Harry Ferguson*, (John Murray, 1972)

Robert Gibbings: *Coming Down the Wye* (Dent, 1942) and *Till I End My Song* (Dent, 1957) by permission of Laurence Pollinger Ltd and the estate of Robert Gibbings

Lilias Rider Haggard: extracts from *Norfolk Life* (Faber, 1943) and from *A Norfolk Notebook* (Faber, 1946) by permission of the publisher; 'Widow Early', from *The Countryman Anthology* (Arthur Barker, 1962), by permission of the editor of *The Countryman*

Maurice H. Harland: 'Pheasant versus Bishop', *(Third Field Bedside*, David & Charles, 1972) by permission of the editor of *The Field*

Mrs Robert Henrey: *Siege of London* (Dent, 1946)

William Holland: *Paupers and Pig Killers* (Alan Sutton 1984)

Dorothy Kahan: 'Work to Rule' from *The Countryman Anthology* (Arthur Barker, 1962) by permission of the editor of *The Countryman*

Francis Kilvert: two extracts from *Diaries*, Vol. 2 (Jonathan Cape, 1939) by permisison of Jonathan Cape and Mrs Sheila Hooper

Fred Kitchen: *The Farming Front* (Dent, 1943)

Juliette de Bairacli Levy: *As Gypsies Wander* (Faber 1953)

Kingsley Martin: *Critic's London Diary* (Secker & Warburg 1960), by permission of David Higham Associates Ltd

H.J. Massingham: *Shepherd's Country* (Chapman & Hall, 1938); *World Without End* (Cobden Sanderson, 1932); *A Countryman's Journal* (Chapman & Hall, 1939), by permission of The Society of Authors as the literary representative of the estate of H.J. Massingham

Spike Mays: *Reuben's Corner* (Methuen, 1969)

Daphne Moore: extract from 'Reminiscences of the Tenth Duke of Beaufort' (1986), by permission of the author and the editor of *Gloucestershire – The County Magazine*)

John Moore: two extracts from *A Walk Through Surrey* (Chapman & Hall, 1939) and *The Cotswolds* (Chapman & Hall, 1937) by permission of Mrs Lucile Bell

Elsie Olivey: 'Christmas at a Village School', by permission of the author

Crichton Porteous: *Farmer's Creed* (Harrap, 1938)

Clifton Reynolds: two extracts from *Glory Hill Farm, (Second year)* (The Bodley Head, 1943)

Benjamin Ryecroft: 'Cattle Trample a Fox, (*Field Bedside Book*, Robson, 1984) by permission of the editor of *The Field*

John Skinner: three extracts from *Journal of a Somerset Rector, 1803-1834* (Oxford University Press, 1984) by permission of Peter Coombs

Sydney Smith: *Selected Letters of Sydney Smith* (Oxford University Press, 1981)

B.A. Steward: *One Journey* (published by the author, 1981), by permission of the author

G.M.L.T.: 'The Constable's Tale' (1935), by permission of the editor of *The Countryman*

Harold Taylor: 'When a Fox Barked', (*Field Bedside Book*, Robson 1984) by permission of the editor of *The Field*

Cecil Torr: two extracts from *Small Talk at Wreyland* (Oxford University Press, 1979)

Brian Vesey-Fitzgerald: two extracts from *A Country Chronicle* (Chapman & Hall, 1942), by permission of Laurence Pollinger Ltd and the estate of Brian Vesey-Fitzgerald

Doreen Wallace: *English Lakeland* (Batsford, 3rd edition, 1948)

C. Henry Warren: *A Boy in Kent* (Bles, 1937); *A Cotswold Year* (Bles, 1936); *The Land Is Yours* (Eyre & Spottiswoode, 1944), by permission of Laurence Pollinger Ltd and the estate of C. Henry Warren

Lewis Wilshire: four extracts from *The Vale of Berkeley* (Robert Hale, 1954)

William Wood: *A Sussex Farmer* (Cape, 1938)

James Woodforde: four extracts from *Diary of a Country Parson* (Oxford University Press 1935/1978)

Dorothy Wordsworth: *Journals* (Oxford University Press, 1958/1971)

Jill Warwick: 'A Faux Pas', by permission of the author

Some copyright owners have been difficult to trace. To those few from whom I have failed to obtain permission, or any I have inadvertently omitted from the list of acknowledgements, I tender my sincere apologies.

The line drawings were prepared by Bill Wright.

# Farming

# The Pleasures of a Country Life

You ask me, what have I been doing? To the best of my memory, what has passed since I came home is as follows:

Finding the roof bad, I sent slaters, at the peril of their necks, to repair it. They mended three holes, and made thirty themselves.

I pulled down as many walls round the house as would have fortified a town. This was in summer; but now, that winter is come, I would give all the money to put them up again, that it cost me to take them down.

I thought it would give a magnificent air to the hall, to throw the passage into it. After it was done, I went out of town to see how it looked. It was night when I went into it; the wind blew out the candle from the over-size of the room; upon which I ordered the partition to be built up again, that I might not die of cold in the midst of summer.

I ordered the old timber to be thinned; to which, perhaps, the love of lucre a little contributed. The workmen, for every tree they cut, destroyed three, by letting them fall on each other. I received a momentary satisfaction from hearing that the carpenter I employed had cut his thumb in felling of a tree. But this pleasure was soon allayed, when, upon examining his measure, I found that he had measured false, and cheated me of 20 per cent.

Instead of saddle-horses I bought mares, and had them covered with an Arabian. When I went, some months after, to mount them, the groom told me, I should kill the foals; and, now I walk on foot, with the stable full of horses, unless when, with much humility, I ask to be admitted into chaise, which is generally refused me.

Remembering, with a pleasing complacency, the Watcombe pigs, I paid thirty shillings for a sow with pig. My wife starved them. They ran over to a madman, called Lord Adam Gordon, who destrained them for damage; and the mother, with ten helpless infants, died of bad usage.

Loving butter much, and cream more, I bought two Dutch cows, and had plenty of both. I made my wife a present of two more: she learned the way to market for their produce; and I have never got a bowl of cream since.

I made a fine hay-stack; but quarrelled with my wife as to the manner of drying the hay, and building the stack. The hay-stack took fire; by which I had the double mortification of losing my hay, and finding my wife had more sense than myself.

I kept no plough; for which I thank my Maker; because then I must have wrote this letter from a gaol.

I paid twenty pounds for a dung-hill, because I was told it was a good thing; and, now, I would give any body twenty shillings to tell me what to do with it.

I built, and stocked a pigeon-house; but the cats watched below, the hawks hovered above; and pigeon soup, roasted pigeon, or cold pigeon-pie, have I never seen since.

I fell to drain a piece of low ground behind the house; but I hit upon the tail of the rock, and drained the well of the house; by which I can get no water for my victuals.

I entered into a great project for selling lime, upon a promise from one of my own farmers to give me land off his farm. But when I went to take off the ground, he laughed, said he had choused the Lawyer, and exposed me to a dozen law-suits for breach of bargains, which I could not perform.

I fattened black cattle and sheep, but could not agree with the butchers about the price. From mere economy, we eat them ourselves, and almost killed all the family with surfeits.

I bought two score of six year old wethers for my own table; but a butcher, who rented one of the fields, put my mark upon his own carrion sheep; by which I have been living upon carrion all the summer.

I brewed much beer; but the small turned sour, and the servants drank all the strong.

I found a ghost in the house, whose name was McAllister, a pedlar, that had been killed in one of the rooms at the top of the house two centuries ago. No servant would go on an errand after the sun was set, for fear of McAllister, which obliged me to set off one set of my servants. Soon after the housekeeper, your old friend Mrs Brown died, aged 90; and then the belief ran, that another ghost was in the house, upon which many of the new set of servants begged leave to quit the house, and got it.

In one thing only have I succeeded. I have quarrelled with all my neighbours; so that, with a dozen gentleman's seats in my view, I stalk alone like a lion in a desert.

I thought I could be happy with my tenants, because I could be insolent to them without their being insolent to me. But they paid me no rent; and in a few days I shall have above one half of the very few friends I have in the country in a prison.

Such being the pleasures of a country life, I intend to quit them all in about a month, to submit to the mortification of spending the Spring in London.

Sir John Dalrymple, Bart.
Letter to Admiral Dalrymple, 1 January 1772

# Wage Rise

The Sussex farmer's boy has a very subtle complex, difficult to get at. You can never tell how fresh events, fresh situations, are going to affect him. When the Agricultural Wages Committee was set up, and the first minimum wage for the agricultural worker established, I heard of a case which demonstrates this very effectively. It happened on the farm of a man I knew farming at Henfield. He paid his men every Friday night, and paid them himself. On the first Friday night that the new wages were to be paid, and they were considerably higher than had ever been paid before, he started to pay first an old man who had worked on the farm nearly all his life. 'Well, Jim, you ain't so young as you were, but this wages committee have fixed the proper wage to be paid to all farm hands, at so much a week.' (I forget the figure and cannot look it up now.) 'If you are old, you are a good hand, and worth as much as some of the young ones, and so I am going to pay you the same money – here it is.' And he handed it over, half as much again as he had paid him the week before, and rather expected some expression of satisfaction. The old man took the money, turned it over in his hand, looked hard at it and looked hard at his master. 'Oh!' he says, 'I be worth this, be I?' Well then, I give you notice to leave next Saturday night. If I be worth this now I was worth a lot more once, and you've been robbing me for forty years. I won't have no more of it.'

Nothing could move him from this resolution, he left the farm and the house he had been living in all those years. There is much to be said for his point of view, but his prompt reaction to the situation was unexpected and surprising to his old employer.

*A Sussex Farmer*
William Wood (1938)


# 'E

A farmer is called by his men either 'the boss' or 'the guvnor' or 'the master' (now out of date), or 'the old man' (regardless of age), or more simply 'he'. He is never called 'the chief'.

At this farm he was sometimes called 'the boss', often enough 'the old man', generally 'He', or, more properly, ''E', and sometimes merely 'the Van'. He used a second-hand butcher's van for getting about the premises and carrying oil and what not from one scene of operation to another. So one would hear – 'Look out, there's the van!' or 'I didn't see no van' when his whereabouts was doubtful. But on the whole he was designated simply as 'E –' 'E's coming!' It is as 'E that I think of him, and as 'E that I shall refer to him.

He was a man somewhere in the fifties. His eyes were impressive in their mildness, but his mouth was large and ugly, partly concealed by a stumpy moustache. You could recognise him a long way off by his walk. He took huge strides, head bent slightly down, like a man measuring a cricket pitch. That walk was very characteristic. There was no dawdling nor diddling about with him: he never strolled; he never looked round quietly at the scene; he never took out a pipe nor smoked a cigarette, any more than he would be likely to drink a glass of beer, pat a dog, or say goodnight, good morning, or thank you. He was on the go the whole time, as if his life depended on it. When he was at all excited, or indeed when giving instructions, he waved his hands about almost like a man catching invisible balls. Though sturdy to a degree, he was obviously a man of nervous temperament.

He came of a farming family for generations back. He had

climbed that famous 'farming ladder' by the only way it can be climbed – by ceaseless energy, relentless toil, and knowledge of the job. Starting with nothing he now ran this large farm with full equipment. Men who rose by their own efforts in farming between 1900 and 1940, and did not fail during the agricultural depression, had to be unusual men. Whatever else 'E was he was not usual, and not small.

Having adopted a certain pace – a terrific pace – he meant to keep it up. He neither would nor could slow down a bit. "E'll break up one of these days' they would say at intervals. He did not intend to lose a minute if he could help it – for time was money to him as certainly as to any business man. An atmosphere of hurry and almost of crisis prevailed whenever he was around; and he generally was around, for he was his own foreman. He was also one of his own labourers, so to speak, for he joined in anything and everything, no job was beneath him. In his way he got a tremendous amount of work out of his men, as he set the pace, and each person felt that he had his eye on him – and he had.

We assembled in the yard in the morning at 7 a.m. There was no question of a good morning any more than of a good evening at the end of the day, nor any degree of cheerfulness. Life was too earnest for that. Orders would be given, and all dispersed in their several directions as quickly as possible out of his sight.

John Stewart Collis
*While Following the Plough* (1946)

# A Critical Moment

Most of my hoeing was done in company with the others. Working at this job in company is not only better for the labourers but better for the farmer – far more ground is covered by a worker in company with others than if alone. The spirit of competition always enters into it, for no one likes to be left behind if the work is being done in paralleled rows as is usual. Thus the pace is according to the fastest worker. And if just two people are taking a couple of rows there is the same tendency to compete, – no one knows why. Once I did this absolutely deliberately. One of 'E's daughters often came out into the fields, and also imitated her father in every particular. Finding myself on a parallel row with her, I worked during the greater part of a morning at an absurd rate, continually passing her as I went up and down the rows.

Harold, Dick and I did a good deal of hoeing together. 'Anyway, it's a bit of a change and break for you,' I said to Harold. 'Yes, but the wrong kind of change,' he replied. All the same he always worked the quickest at this job as at many others. We were working now on a field along which the main track ran. Hence the approach of the Van was easily seen. When it was discerned approaching, our pace would quicken; not too fast, since that would look bad, too obvious; but appreciably, while we asked 'Is 'E going to stop?' If the Van stopped then we might expect 'E to alight and come across, look on, make a criticism, and possibly join us. Thus it was always a critical moment when the Van was seen – 'Will 'E stop, join us, and spoil the morning?' became the great question. One occasion was rather amusing. Harold, Dick and myself were going along our rows side by side across the field. Our cut reached to about the middle of the field, when normally we would turn about. We were working towards the track when the Van appeared coming up, and then stopped. 'E got out and went over into the next field to speak to Robert, and there he remained for some time. We couldn't see him, but had to suppose that he could see us. At last he appeared again. Would he now come over to us? But no, he got into the van. But it didn't start off at once; evidently he was watching us. We were all working towards the track, towards him. We came to the end of our cut. We should now have stopped, picked our new rows and gone back. But Harold said, 'Keep on, don't stop, keep on; if 'e sees us stop 'E'll come over, sure thing. Keep on and e'll b off.' And though we had come to the end of our cut we kept going now on ground which we had already hoed ('E wouldn't be able to notice this at the distance), and continued keeping on until the crisis passed and 'E got back into the van and did at last b off.

John Stewart Collis<br>While Following the Plough (1946)

# Left, Right and Wrong

We harnessed the horses; we ploughed, peeling sticks, pacing and aligning. That high hedge screened us from the road. Mr Colville walked over while we were at it, and stood looking thoughtful. But in the end he said, 'You ain't making a bad job of that, not at all you ain't.' We sorted out his negatives and were highly pleased. The hedge could now come down; the village could see our four acres of ploughing and welcome.

I had two billhooks which I had bought among other odd lots at a Michaelmas sale. Frank and I each chose one, and set about the hedge. It was the hedging season. Everywhere we went we observed those clean, almond-shaped cuts all over stubs of hazel and thorn; smooth butter-coloured ovals, with no frayed edges to the bark – signs of expert work with keen tools.

We honed our bills, we swung at the hedge, we honed again. We fell to with redoubled vigour; yet nothing we could do would persuade our blades to slice off even a middling sized stick of that hedge at one blow. We hewed and hacked. Our bills bounced. The stubs began to look as though a tiger had been sharpening its claws on them. In the pub villagers accosted us 'You're making a funny mess o' that hedge o' yours, masters.' I can still hear the lilt of the words and the word 'masters' rising falsetto to the verge of a cackle.

And the cutting, arduous as it was, was still only half the job. We had omitted the precaution of separating our cuttings as we worked. When we had done we found that our hedge was still a hedge, cut off at the roots but entangled all together. We strained and heaved at it with long-handled forks. We reared great tents of bramble and briar over us to try to drag to our bonfire. A bramble would slip off the tines, and down the whole lot would descend on our heads, faces, shoulders, arms. We helped each other out of these prickly cages, rolled them over the fire, jumped on them to depress them on to the flames, and when they flared, leaped off with singed eyebrows.

'A pretty sight we'll look at the dance,' we said. There was to be a Christmas dance at Frank's parents' big house in the suburb where both his parents and mine lived.

Just as we were finishing the hedge, Mr Colville, who had praised our ploughing, and had heard about the 'funny mess' we were making of that hedge, came along to see what we were up to. He looked at our tools, felt their edges.

'Can't make it out,' he said, surveying the bristly gashes on the stubs. He looked again at my billhook. Suddenly he cried, 'Dash it, this is a left-handed bill. It's made for a man who works with his left hand. You see, it's ground so that the bevel is on the other side; so of course if you used it right-handed it would keep jumping off the work.'

He put the two bills together to show us the difference, saying as he did so, 'But I can't make out why Frank didn't get on better with his.'

'I can,' I told him. 'Frank is left-handed.'

Adrian Bell
*My Own Master* (1961)

# The Butcher and the Grazier

A few years before, being at Barnett Fair, I saw a battle going on, arising out of some sudden quarrel, between a Butcher, and the servant of a West-country Grazier. The Butcher, though vastly superior in point of size, finding that he was getting the worst of it, recoiled a step or two, and drew out his knife. Upon the sight of this weapon, the Grazier turned about and ran off till he came up to a Scotchman who was guarding his herd, and out of whose hand the former snatched a good ash stick about four feet long. Having thus got what he called a long arm, he returned to the combat, and, in a very short time, he gave the Butcher a blow upon the wrist which brought his knife to the ground. The Grazier then fell to work with his stick in such a style as I had never before witnessed. The Butcher fell down and rolled and kicked; but, he seemed only to change his position in order to insure to every part of his carcase a due share of the penalty of his baseness. After the Grazier had, apparently, tired himself, he was coming away, when, happening to cast his eye upon the knife, he ran back and renewed his basting, exclaiming every now and then, as he caught his breath: 'dra' they knife wo't!' till at last the Butcher was so bruised that he was actually unable to stand, or even to get up; and yet, such amongst Englishmen was the abhorrence of foul fighting, that not a soul attempted to interfere, and nobody seemed to pity a man thus unmercifully beaten. It was my intention to imitate the conduct of this Grazier; to resort to a long arm, by going to America, and to combat Corruption while I kept myself out of the reach of her knife. Nobody called the Grazier a coward because he did not stay to oppose his fists to a pointed and cutting instrument.

William Cobbett
*Political Register*, 29 March 1817

## Laying up Ridges

The high lands of the vale of Evesham have long been proverbial. Those of the vale of Gloucester are equally entitled to notoriety. It has been said of them, hyperbolically, that men on horseback, riding in the furrows, could not see each other over the ridges. This, we may venture to say, was never the case; though heretofore, perhaps, they may have been higher than they are at present. Not many years ago, there was an instance of ridges, toward the centre of this vale, which were so high, that two men above the middle size, standing in the furrows, could not see each other's heads; I have, myself, stood in the furrow of a wheat stubble; the tips of which, upon the ridges, rose to the eye: a man, somewhat below the middle size, accidentally crossing them, sunk below the sight in every furrow he descended into. But the stubble, in this instance, was not less than eighteen inches high. The height of soil from four feet to four feet three inches: – the width of these lands about fifteen yards. – I afterwards measured a furrow near four feet deep.

But an anecdote, relative to the first mentioned ridges, will shew these extraordinary moments of human industry in a more striking light, than any dimensions which can be given. The occupier of them had, at a pinch, occasion to borrow some plow-teams of his friends; one of whom called upon him, in the course of the day, to see them at work, and was directed to the field, where six or seven teams were plowing. He went to the field (a flat inclosure of twelve or fifteen acres) but seeing nothing of the teams, he concluded he had mistaken the direction, and went back for a fresh one. The fact was, the several teams were making up their furrows, and were wholly hid, by the ridges, from his sight.

William Marshall
*Rural Economy of Gloucestershire* (1789)

# Sticklebacks

These little fish which are caught in immense quantities in the Lynn rivers about once in seven years, have been bought as high as 8d. a bushel. The favourite way of using them now, is by mixing with mould and carrying on for turnips. Great quantities have been carried to Marham, Shouldham and Beachamwell. Mr. Fuller there, is reported to have laid out £400 for them in one year: they always answer exceedingly.

Mr. Rogerson, of Narborough, has gone largely into this husbandry, laying out £300 in one year, at from 6d. to 8d. a bushel, besides carriage from Lynn: he formed them into composts with mould, mixed well by turning over, and carried on for turnips: the success was great.

Arthur Young
*General View of the Agriculture of the County of Norfolk* (1804)

# Haymaking, 1828

The people in the hayfield, who had had a double potation of cider, were not, however, contented; but just as I was stepping into bed, the servant knocked at my door to say that they were come for more. I desired her to tell them to go home, that I was sure they had had too much already, and that my parsonage was not a pothouse. My life is indeed become a burden. In order to supply employment for my wounded spirit I occupied the whole morning in tinting sketches I have lately taken. This employed me till dinner-time, after which I took up one of the volumes of Mountfacon, and had just applied myself to reading when my servant, George, came to the parlour door giving a violent knock and saying that the people had no drink in the hayfield. George also said he had been working all day without beer, and could do so no longer. I asked why he had not gotten any. 'Because,' he said, 'the barrel is out!' I asked what he wanted me to do; they were such a set of gormondising gluttons, they never were content; that they had sent for cider last night, when I was just going to bed: that I had granted them cider as well as beer because I thought they would get in my hay before dark; on going to the field I found they had not done so. I said that if they had drunk up all the beer I could not help it; how can I get beer at a moment's notice? But he should have his wish – that he might take the horse and cart and go to White's at Red Hill, and get an 18-gallon cask of small beer, such as was drunk in my family: and if he did not like that, he might leave me; if he imagined that I thought him of any value he was mistaken: I had done much for him, and had met with the same ingratitude I had done from others.

John Skinner
*Journal of a Somerset Rector, 1803–1834* (1984 edition)

# The Reverend Sydney Smith, Farmer

It has been my lot to have passed the greater part of my life in cities. – About six or seven years ago, I was placed in the country, in a situation where I was under the necessity of becoming a farmer; and, amongst the many expensive blunders I have made, I warn those who may find themselves in similar situations, against Scotch Sheep and Oxen for ploughing. I had heard a great deal of the fine flavour of scotch mutton, and it was one of the great luxuries I promised myself in farming. A luxury certainly it is; but the price paid for it is such, that I would rather give up the use of animal food altogether, than obtain it by such a system of cares and anxieties. Ten times a day my men were called off from their work to hunt the Scotch sheep out of my own or my neighbour's wheat. They crawled through hedges where I should have thought a rabbit could hardly have found admission; and, where crawling would not do, they had recourse to leaping. Five or six times they all assembled, and set out on their return to the North. My bailiff took a place in the mail, pursued, and overtook them half way to Newcastle. Then it was quite impossible to get them fat. They consumed my turnips in winter, and my clover in the summer, without any apparent addition to their weight; 10 or 12 per cent. always died of the rot; and more would have perished in the same manner, if they had not been prematurely eaten out of the way.

My ploughing oxen were an equal subject of vexation. They had a constant purging upon them, which it was impossible to stop. They ate more than twice as much as the same number of horses. They did half as much work as the same number of horses. They could not bear hot weather, nor wet weather, nor go well down hill. It took five men to shoe an ox. They ran against my gate posts, lay down in the cart whenever they were tired, and ran away at the sight of a stranger.

I have now got into a good breed of English sheep, and useful cart-horses, and am doing very well. I make this statement to guard young gentlemen farmers against listening to the pernicious nonsense of brother gentlemen, for whose advice I am at least poorer by 3001 or 4001.

Sydney Smith, August 1819
*Selected Letters of Sydney Smith* (1981)

# Wool Storage

A story is told of a cunning wool buyer in the dim past weighing up wool on an upper floor of some farm premises. As the fleeces passed the machine they were thrown down an opening to the floor beneath in readiness for packing. The pile of wool upstairs had been there for some time and was full of rats. As the fleeces were moved a rat would sometimes rush out trying to escape. No farm labourer can resist a rat hunt, so the buyer being left alone beside the still unmoved fleeces, whenever a rat appeared, and the men scattered in every direction in pursuit, he took the opportunity to kick a few fleeces unweighed down the opening. When the owner came to reckon the quantity the buyer should have had, and compared it with the weight, the fraud was discovered, and the deficiency had to be made good.

I heard of a Hampshire farmer whose wife was anxious for a drawing-room to be added to an inadequate farmhouse, and the tenant with some difficulty persuaded the landlord to make the alteration. When the work was complete the farmer expressed the great satisfaction of his wife and himself with the addition, and the landlord was anxious to see the new room. Every time he suggested a day, the farmer objected that it would be inconvenient to his wife, or that he himself would be away from home. Time went on, and the landlord, finding it impossible to arrange a day that was not objected to, made a surprise visit, when shooting over the farm. The farmer protested as to the inconvenience, but the owner insisted, and was conducted to the new drawing-room. The door was thrown open, and the room was seen to be stacked from floor to ceiling with wool, without a stick of furniture in the place!

Arthur H. Savory
*Grain and Chaff from an English Manor* (1920)

# The Shepherd's Tale

On a wet and misty day in the Fells of the Lake Country the shepherd and his son went out to collect their flock of some 800 sheep and bring them down to the lower ground. They rounded up as many as they could find under the handicap of the day's darkness, but when they came to 'tell the tale' (which is still good English for counting the number) the flock was short by some hundred and thirty head. The man and boy then sat down to make an estimate, by name and descriptive title of the missing. The shepherd soon completed a list that proved to be only seven short, and his son missed the due sum by about twice the number.

It would seem even to most countrymen, a scarcely credible achievement that a man should be able to distinguish and name the numbers of his great flock even if he had them in front of his very eyes. That he should perceive exactly which individual sheep were missing will seem 'scarcely human' (as the old lady said of the hippopotamus at the Zoo). A feat such as this of the

Lake shepherd and his son, wonderful enough in itself, is eloquent of the real significance of a phrase, often lightly used: 'farming is a way of life.'

Sir William Beach Thomas
*A Year in the Country* (1950)

# Poultry Problems

Mr Tope, one of the older poultry farmers near here, knows his business, his speciality is a first cross for the table; a widower, he works with his grandson. Here is a little record of two conversations.

The Scribe: 'Have youna dozen good birds four to five pounds that you can let me have at the rate of one, perhaps two, a week?'

Mr Tope: 'I can't do that for ye. Tell ye f'r why. Chickens is bound to rise. If I ast ye to-day's price I'd be robbin' meself every week. Everybody wants a good chicken.'

The Scribe: 'But prices may fall. They do after the summer season. London doesn't buy much after July.'

Mr Tope: 'You don't want to tell me. Prices'll be high along o' the weather we bin an' had these past years. You'd better come here every week an' I'll treat ye fair.'

The Scribe: 'But will you keep the birds for me?'

Mr Tope: 'If so be I can. Nut I can't get half the birds I want. I don't get no peace o' me life along o' folks askin' me for 'em.'

A little later in the same week a man I know told me he was giving up his poultry because he is too busy to attend to them and the flock is too small to carry a paid worker. I advised him to go to Mr Tope and offer his young table birds for finishing. Here so far as I can gather is what Mr Tope told him.

'Everybody's trying to sell chickens but nobody wants to see one. They're no trade to-day. Folks grumble at a fair price. They'll go down every week, will chickens, mark my words if they don't. Trade's all right up to July. After that they tell me fash'nable folk won't look at a chicken, if youn were to bring it to them ready cooked. I've more birds than I know what to do with. But there, I'll give ten pence a pound an' I'll lose money on them, sure as harvest.'

There is matter for satisfaction in the thought that one of Mr Tope's prophecies must justify him.

S.L. Bensusan
*Back of Beyond* (1945)

# A Clever Auctioneer

It recalls to me another plea for bad farming, as quaint, but far more ingenious, which I heard many years ago from a Notts auctioneer, the cleverest of his craft in the midland counties. He was offering for sale a farm in our neighbourhood, which had been long neglected by idle and impoverished tenants, when one of his audience proclaimed in a loud voice, 'that he wouldn't have the place as a gift that it was more like a dockyard than a farm, and he didn't think it would produce a new corn from an old one.' The auctioneer heard him patiently, and when he had concluded his disparagements, he replied to the effect 'that he should make no attempt to conceal the fact that the farm was not in a satisfactory condition; but the land itself was excellent, and he was sure that any occupier possessed of the intelligence of the gentleman who had just favoured them with his candid and gratuitous remarks' (hereupon all eyes were fixed on the commentator to his evident discomfort) 'any tenant with his quick discovery of defects, his knowledge of draining' (the sale took place on the afternoon of a market day, and the countenance of the critic, who had just come from 'the ordinary', was still aglow with alcoholic fire) 'would speedily restore order, fertility and abundance. And I think,' he continued, 'that this gentleman has not duly considered the present advantages, as well as the future profits, to be derived from a farm such as this which I have now the honour of offering to your notice. I would ask you to reflect for a moment upon the temptations which beset a young man who has entered upon a farm on which everything has been done which capital and culture could do. He goes out to find that no repairs are required, no improvements can be designed, no alteration can be made in the regular routine of work. So he returns to his home, has a glass of brandy-and-water, and smokes a cigar.

Takes another walk after his dinner; same results – more brandy-and-water, more cigars; contracts a habit of drinking, loses his money, loses his health, dies in the workhouse! Whereas a young man who takes the tenancy of the farm which is now on sale is compelled to be industrious, and has not a moment of spare time upon his hands; his active habits make him healthful, a beautiful wife and lovely children make his home happy, frugality makes him rich, and he dies at an advanced age, respected by all, and bequeathing a thousand pounds to the Nottingham Infirmary.' After this introduction the speaker, having put all his hearers but one in good humour, proceeded to business.

*The Memories of Dean Hole* (Nelson, c. 1900)

# The Cattle-Dealer

My friend, the late Mr Archibald Scott, the estate agent whom we employed, was one of the leading men in his profession; and a man of great ability. He told me the following true story.

One of the dealers who attended his market regularly, came to him one autumn and said that he wanted to buy some heifers. For this purpose he wanted to raise money from the auctioneer on the agreement that he would sell these heifers in Mr Scott's market in the following spring. This is a usual arrangement. Mr Scott agreed and the dealer having signed the necessary documents, bought the bunch of heifers for three hundred pounds.

From time to time the dealer was asked about the heifers and he always said that they were doing well. When spring came he told Mr Scott that he had decided to put the heifers to the bull and sell them, in due course, as springers.

Mr Scott began to get suspicious and said to the dealer: 'I'd like to have a look at those heifers. Where are they?'

He replied that they were on the fens near Methwold, some miles away, and he added: 'If you're going to see them, let me know or maybe you may not find them as they are on an offhand farm.'

Time went on and the heifers were not brought for sale in Mr

Scott's market. So finally he drew the dealer aside one day and said: 'Look here, I realise I have lost my money, but just tell me exactly what has happened and how you swindled me.'

The dealer replied: 'It's this way, Mr Scott. You have never been in a position where you had to have three hundred pounds at once. Now when I found myself in that position I thought of my old friend Mr Scott. I bought these heifers in the market and put them again through in the same market. I lost half a crown a head on the deal; but don't you worry – you will be paid.' It's no good crying over spilt milk so Mr Scott faced the loss.

But curiously enough some six months later the dealer came and paid him off in full.

'Where did you get the money from?' he asked.

'Well, I knew I couldn't get the money no other way, so I advertised for a wife and got married.'

'What did you say in your advertisement?'

'Well, I reckoned it was no good beating about the bush; so I advertised for a wife with money. I made an appointment where to meet. And when I got there, there was three women. I chose the most likely one and I married her; and here is your money.'

What particularly appealed to Mr Scott was the way in which, when the dealer wanted to swindle someone, he went as he said to his old friend Mr Scott.

Justin and Edith Brooke
*Suffolk Prospect* (1963)

# Another Dealer

A young cow had come to me covered, as it were, with medals. Her ancestry was fine, but she had been a failure in her first lactation period. Apart from this she was not much to look at. I went with her to market because I was told it is much better for the owner to show his face and to be there to answer questions.

I stood by the cow as instructed while she was waiting her turn.

'T.T.?'

'Yes, certainly,' I replied.

'Easy milker?'

'Try her.'

'What do you reckon she'll fetch?'

'Forty-five.'

'You'd be lucky.'

'What do you put her at?' I asked.

'I'll give you thirty-five.'

'Nothing doing.' I knew I would be well rid of her for £35, but I waited.

Along came someone I knew. 'Would you like me to try to sell her privately before the sale?' he asked.

'What would you want out of it?'

'Ten bob.'

'All right. I'll give you ten bob if you can make forty pounds of her.'

He brought along a buyer who tried very hard to beat me down. Finally I let her go for £38.10s. He gave me the money on the spot and I paid out the 10s., leaving £38 clear. I was satisfied.

'Who is this chap?' I asked my friend.

'Oh, just a dealer. He's always here.'

'What will he do with her?'

'Run her through the sale, I expect. He wants a price ticket he can show to a client.'

'You mean he'll buy her himself at a higher price, so that he can have documentary evidence of what she cost him?'

'That's the idea. The ticket will have your name on it.'

'Does that mean I shall have to pay the auctioneer's commission?'

'No, he'll do that. I expect he'll get Old Jim to run her up. Maybe someone will get caught.'

I watched what would happen. I asked the dealer who had bought my cow if he really was going to run her through the market. He pretended to be indifferent about it. I begged him to do it, for my sake, as a favour. He condescendingly agreed. I saw him whispering to Old Jim.

'Old Jim,' I was told hurriedly by my friend, 'is a character who is 50 per cent of this market. He is very rich, he's always here, and everyone follows his lead. You watch him when your cow comes up.'

When finally she entered the ring I stood by my friend who had the ten shillings. The man who often jumped into the ring and felt the udders, who winked and made witty remarks, and whose privileges I had previously resented as unfair, did it all now.

'Who's he?' I asked.

'Jim's man.'

The bidding went up steadily.

'Forty pun ten, fife, fife, fife, what a bag ten, ten, fifteen here, come on, no price at all, forty-one, thank you, over there.'

The familiar auctioneer's yapping went on.

'Forty-three-five – ten – fifteen – forty-four.' Still they were bidding briskly.

'Forty-fife. Forty-fife pounds I'm bid for this fine cow from Mr Reynolds of Glory Hill. Tuberculin test certificate in my hand dated less than a month ago. Have you all finished at forty-fife? Thank you, Sir. Forty-fife, fife, I'm bid. Any advance? Ten, thank you.' They were off again.

Finally she reached £46.10s. The same price as the cow which cost me £18, but this one had cost me £28 as a heifer. I looked at the man who had paid me £38.10s. He seemed pleased.

'Did he buy her in, or was she really sold?' I asked my friend.

He went over to inquire. When he came back and told me she had really been sold I looked up and caught the eye of the man who had bought her from me. He smiled triumphantly. He had earned £8 in a few minutes and had his fun for nothing. I asked my friend what Old Jim got out of this.

'About a quid, I expect.'

That's how it's done. Next time I went to market I got into touch with Old Jim direct.

'Help me for a quid?' I said.

'Show me the cow,' he said.

I showed him.

He explained his risk. 'I can't run her up unreasonable,' he said. 'I don't want to be landed with a dud for the sake of a quid.'

'You know when to drop out,' I said.

'Maybe I do. Still, it's a risk. You mustn't open your mouth too wide. How much will you really be satisfied with, Mister?'

The situation merely resolved itself into selling the cow to Old Jim himself, but I did not realise it at the time. However, we went through all the motions: I heard the bidding; I watched

Old Jim: I had my fun and I think I made a little more than I should have done without Old Jim's assistance. But I am not sure because the cow was bought by a perfect stranger at a fair price. I didn't see Old Jim do anything and perhaps I paid him a pound for nothing.

Clifton Reynolds
*Glory Hill Farm (Second Year)* (1943)

# Buying a Couple of Pigs

The notice on the tumbledown wall read: 'Pure New Honey'. The gate was off its hinges and I had difficulty in opening it. Grass grew in the cracks between the paving stones that led to the front door, and the stones were green with slime.

The drab paint on the door was blistered and peeling. I knocked. At a window a grimy curtain twitched, and after some scuffling the door opened wide enough for a head to poke out.

'You'll have come about the pigs,' said the head. I nodded and the door opened wide enough to reveal an old woman. Grey, that's the only way to describe her, not only her hair and clothes, but her whole appearance and demeanour – just grey. I followed her through the neglected garden, rotting cabbages, sprout stalks, brambles, docks and nettles. The plot was littered with upturned rusty buckets, presumably for forcing rhubarb. We clambered over an old iron hurdle, and I wondered how the old woman managed. She must have noticed my look, for she spoke again.

'Yes, twice a day I've got to carry buckets of pig food over here. It's not good enough. He promises to put me a gate, but as you see, he doesn't.'

I agreed that it did not seem good enough, and a gate was certainly needed.

We were now out in a field littered with all manner of items, mostly junk. She told me that 'he' was not at home, but was most likely in the Green Man or the Wagon and Horses. In the middle of the field was a shed, beyond which the field sloped steeply up to a high hedge. It surprised me slightly when a bicycle suddenly came hurtling over the top of this; even more so when a figure appeared crawling through the undergrowth.

It stood up to be revealed as a small man with very baggy trousers and a large moustache, who promptly started to run down the slope, his knees coming up almost to his chin. 'That's him and he's drunk,' I was told.

With deep blue eyes twinkling, he passed us smiling and waving. 'Can't stop, see you soon,' he sang out, disappearing behind some brambles.

In silence we awaited his return, but instead he ignored us and went straight inside the hovel. After a few minutes I heard his voice and thinking it was an invitation to go inside, I did so.

It was gloomy in there, and I couldn't see him at first, but as I grew accustomed to the darkness, I spied him lying alongside a big Saddleback sow, playing with and talking to her piglets.

'There then, my little beauties. Oh, my little darlings.' He took not the slightest notice of me, but continued to fondle the pigs.

After a while, I grew rather tired of this for a caper, and told him I had come to buy a couple of the young gilts. He looked up at me with a radiant smile, 'Ah, but I don't know as I want to sell 'em.'

'But you advertised them in the paper,' I exclaimed.

This had him nonplussed for a while, but eventually he spoke again.

'There's that old sawmill of mine lying idle. Now, you do know that oughta be working.'

This new tactic, in turn, set me back a little, but, as briskly as I could, I returned to the business in hand, and after more inconsequential mutterings, he spoke of the pigs again.

'She's got ten pigs. I think she had eleven and lay on one, because I smelt something nasty under the straw, but I never looked. There's four gilts, and I've sold two of 'em to the Green Man. You can have the other two in a fortnight for eight pound apiece.'

With a dreamy grin he settled back in the straw, lost interest in me, and I left him uttering endearments to his family. It was good to be back in the air again.

On my way back I passed his wife feeding her fowls. She asked if I'd bought any of the pigs.

'Two of the gilts. The others were sold to the Green Man.'

'Oh dear, I wish my pigs weren't going there. They aren't

proper sort of people. I might have guessed it; but they're not what I call proper people at all.'

Humphrey Phelps
*Gloucestershire & Avon Life*, September 1977

# It Wants Greasing

A dealer in agricultural machinery took a beet-cutter to demonstrate to a farmer. The farmer called one of his men and said: 'Here, George, you have a go at it. Tell me what you think on it.' An old worker, after giving the machine a jaundiced look, turned the handle and tried it with a few roots. Asked what he thought of it he said with conviction: 'It's some stiff, maaster. It whoolly sticks when you turn thet wheel: I fare to think it wants greasin'.' 'Send for Copping (the dealer); he's just across the field a-looking at that harrow,' said the farmer. The verdict 'it wants greasin' was repeated to the dealer, but as he was a Suffolk man himself he summed up the situation in a moment. So as soon as the farmer's back was turned he slipped a shilling into the old boy's palm – 'Six pints o' beer at that time o' day' – and said to him: 'Just yew have a go at it now, bo'.' On being asked the second time by the farmer how the machine worked, the old worker said: 'It be whoolly fine now, maaster. It dew go like a rick on fire.'

George Ewart Evans
*Ask the Fellows who Cut the Hay* (2nd edition, 1961)

# Raspberry Picking

'What sort of a crowd to-day?' I asked, for pickers are hard to get and uncertain in their comings and goings. 'Pretty useful,' is the answer. 'The usual locals. Two bus loads and some push-bikes, and more promised. About sixty I should say.' Among the five foot canes of Lloyd George berries one sees only an occasional head and it is difficult to realise that more than half a hundred women are at work.

The pickers each expect a word of greeting, a polite inquiry or a bit of chaff from the boss, so come along and meet them. Some are old-timers, others are newcomers, sometimes relatives down for a holiday who little know what they have let themselves in for. Some are cheery and over-familiar, some are haughty and brook no familiarity, others are chatty and like to share their troubles, recount their complaints, their symptoms and what the doctor said. Here's one little gypsy of a woman, black crinkly hair and a gold ring in each ear. She has a flock of children with her, but they all pick and work like niggers. 'Well, 'Mrs Starling,' I say, 'what about that man of yours? Will he be out in time for the apple picking?' She shakes her head and grimaces. 'Two years this time,' she explains. So far he has usually managed to be out of gaol in the early autumn, but burglary needs more correction than petty larceny, and we must find another picker for this year.

A furtive young female in the next row stops me and explains that the lady three rows off has brought a chopper with her, has spat in her eye and proposes to chop off her head. She wants to go home but has no bus fare. I interview the would-be executioner and tell her that no lady who cuts off another lady's head with a chopper can expect to rate as a raspberry picker. 'I'll give her raspberry the something something,' she declaims. 'Languishin' at my old man,' she adds for my benefit. 'Oh come now,' I seek to pacify her. 'A little languishing now and then doesn't do anyone a bit of harm.' She glares at me and from her bag produces the chopper and work in the immediate neighbourhood stops so that all may listen-in. It is no good. A look in her left eye tells me that there is dirty weather ahead and I return to the 'languisher' and hand her eightpence in exchange for picking tokens to pay her bus fare home.

A sweat-streaked face looks up at me from the next row. 'Coo! sir, it ain't 'arf 'ot,' grumbles the old lady. She is wearing a black wool tam-o'-shanter, a black near-silk scarf round her neck and a black blouse and skirt. She is evidently regarded with great affection by the flies. 'Well,' I say, 'what can you expect if you will come dressed for a funeral? Black is degrees hotter to wear than any light colour.' She does not believe me so I make her lay her hand upon the dark liver marking of my spaniel dog and then upon the white of his coat. The difference in temperature is quite obvious. 'Well, I never did,' she exclaims.

'Mrs Smith, did you know as a dawg was hot one side and cold the other? Fancy that now.' Mrs Smith quite obviously knows nothing of the laws of heat reflections and absorption and I feel that her confirmation of the fact is not needed. I restrain also my desire to tell the old lady that the shape and colour of her hat is responsible for the plague of flies, which mistake it for one of those common ornaments to our main roads following the passage of a herd of cows.

Here Mrs Malbrook, who earns perhaps 3s6d a day, when the day is fine, has a Gloucestershire accent and is convinced that she is of almost royal French descent, asks me for the hundredth time if I will repeat the verse that begins with her name – 'Malbrouk s'en va-t-en guerre' – smiling with justifiable pride as the quite unintelligible doggerel is repeated. She is extremely proud of her ancestor, though not at all sure, or concerned, as to which side of the blanket her descent should be credited.

Oh help! Here are two poor innocents from the town in thin muslin blouses with no sleeves. Already the droop at the corners of both mouths proclaims their weariness with the day scarce begun. Their arms, which at dawn were lily-white, are now an angry shrimp pink. 'We want to get sunburned,' they explain. I shake my head at them and produce a pot of vaseline, carried for the purpose. 'Here, rub it in,' I tell them. 'You can't fry without fat or oil.' We shall not see them again, for the first exposure to a hot July sun in the shelter of a raspberry row is calculated to raise blisters as big as saucers on the arm which is not used to it.

Hullo! There's trouble here. A lady of no uncertain shape is lying in the shade of the hedgerow proclaiming that she is about to become a mother. I had my suspicions regarding her intentions some time ago, now she seems to have made up her mind. This is a case of home, sweet home. I pick a stout and sensible body who I know has at least six little worries of her own and is no amateur, and tell her to get ready to come with us. I bring the car across the field and the sensible body, having assisted the very unwise one into the front seat beside me, climbs into the dicky seat, as, amid a volley of cheers and derisive advice, we begin our pilgrimage of pain to the town eleven miles away.

Raymond Bush
*Fruit Salad* (1947)

# Studying the Seed Catalogue

At the beginning of each season Grandfather sat by the fire with a collection of seed catalogues and worked through them, marking everything he thought he'd like to grow. All the time he consulted Granny.

'Savoy,' he said, 'What about more of they Savoys, Nell? I wants to put cabbage where I had the beans last year, and where I had the cabbage bed, I've a mind to have the beans. And I'll put in a few more turnips. They were good, they turnips we had last year. Didn't you think so, Nell?'

'Give me the scatters,' she said.

'You never said so.'

'No. Well, it wouldn't have done any good.'

He considered what she'd told him. Then he said: 'I don't reckon as it could have bin the turnips. It was summat you picked up in the air, more like. There's any amount going about in the air, springtimes.'

'But I shan't eat no more turnips,' she said decisively.

'You grow 'em, if you want to. There's nothing to stop you and George having 'em if they agrees with you.' He considered the catalogue.

'We'll have some more brock-lo. I likes brock-lo. And that beet we had last year. We'll have some more of that. Good for yer blood, beet is. What do you think about that, then, Matilda?'

'It didn't do my blood much good. Too rich or summat.'

'Well there's no sense in eating what rounds on you, that's for sure. What about carrots? They be all right. You can eat carrots all right, can't you, Nell?'

'Yes. I can eat carrots. And I likes a mess of peas. We could do with some peas, couldn't we, Will?'

'Gives you the wind, Nell ...' he reminded her.

'Yes, I know they do. But I dunno as I mind if you don't.'

Mavis Budd
*Fit For A Duchess* (1970)

# Beasts and Birds of Field and Farm

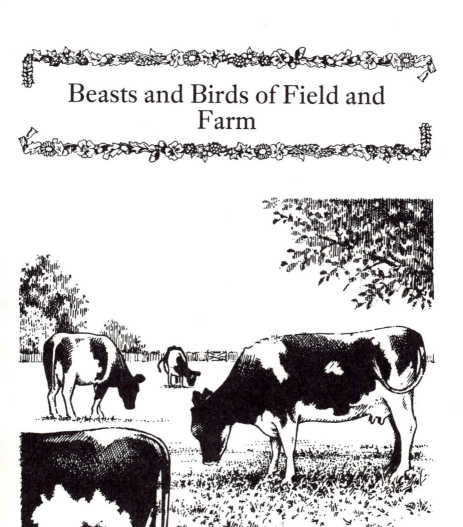

# A Badger's Funeral

I was beginning to wonder, in the nasty manner of human beings, whether the domestic life of the badger was quite blameless, and when the Don Juan of badgers would go, or if he would be caught by an irate husband, and what would happen if he was – in fact my mind was behaving in a thoroughly civilised way – when the visitor reappeared, or at least his tail. Gradually the whole of him came into view. And then I saw that he was dragging something. It was the body of a badger. Had he added murder to his other sins? But no sooner was the body clear of the entrance than the female appeared. At this point I sneezed loudly twice, but neither animal took the slightest notice. Together they dragged the body of the old male across my line of vision to the rabbit warren. The male had hold of the corpse by a hind leg: I could not see how the female was assisting him, but assisting him she was.

In a very short time they had reached the warren. Here, even in the improved light, I was unable to see clearly what was happening. Indeed, though at various moments I made out both badgers. I could not really see what they were doing. It was not hard to guess, however, and soon the indistinct sounds of scratching confirmed my guesses. Father was being buried.

Shortly, they had finished. The service was over. There was no further performance of any kind. No sounds, no noise at all. No more touching, nothing. The male vanished, moving very quickly, the way that he had come. The female came back to her home, stood for a moment at the entrance, looking straight at me as though saying, 'Now, what do you think of that?' and then disappeared below the ground.

It was 4.10. Unnoticed the dawn had broken. Unnoticed the birds had commenced their daily round. Though by no means light, it was much lighter, and I had not observed the passing of time. I waited another half hour, conscious now of chill air and great hunger. But there was no movement from the sett, and at last, lighting my pipe, I went over to examine the warren. Earth had been shovelled into the mouth, and packed by the bodies brushed against it. It would have been easy to loosen the earth and exhume the body inside, but I did not. That would, to me at least, have been sacrilege. I turned away, and, after examining the track, clearly defined, from sett to warren, tramped off home, thrilled and hungry.

Brian Vesey-Fitzgerald
*A Country Chronicle* (1942)

# The Death of a Jackdaw

Details of a remarkable incident associated with the death of a Jackdaw on Bream Down have been forwarded to us by Mr Harry Cox, F.Z.S. the warden. His heading is 'A Bream Down Inquiry and a Fatality.'

It was an unusual case; unusual because the jury sitting upon it was more than the legal number, and the case was heard in the open air, quite near the watcher's hut, but little has been heard about it. The subject of the inquiry was not dead, and it was not very lively, either. It was a very sick jackdaw, and the story is being revived because a radio talk was given on Sunday last about rooks. Do they in the case of a sick member of the community, put it to death? Here's the Bream Down story about a jackdaw which was brought to the watcher's hut by some little girls; the bird was certainly very sick, could anything be done to revive it? Nothing could. The bird was put in a nice quiet spot where it could be revived unmolested if nature so willed it. A few minutes later a number of its compeers, about 50 of them, arrived, and formed a ring around it and the circle gradually closed in on the invalid. The watcher had to catch a bus, so the 'jury' carried on without any outside help. On the watcher's return several hours later, when the jury had dispersed, the subject of the inquiry lay there, quite dead, yet with no sign of injury. Perhaps they had given their verdict. The bird watcher could not make any decision; it was beyond his capability.

*Weston Mercury*
5 March 1949

# Protest Meeting

Some years ago jackdaws were stealing the food from the pigs and poultry in the orchard. Then they started playing havoc with a field of barley. Our efforts to drive them away were greeted with mockery. Enough was enough, the thieving and the plundering, their mockery added insult to injury. Shooting was ineffective, so we made a large cage with a funnelled opening in the roof and put a live jackdaw inside as a decoy.

The other jackdaws, we had been assured, would come and go down the funnel and become trapped. Jackdaws came and peered down the funnelled opening but did not go inside. More jackdaws arrived and paced round the cage, and then flew away to return with yet more jackdaws. They inspected the cage and made angry noises, they strutted and complained loudly. Still more jackdaws arrived, scores multiplied into hundreds and hundreds into thousands; soon the air was black with jackdaws.

They held a mass meeting in the adjoining field, several in turn addressed the meeting, in raucous and no doubt eloquent terms. Then the majority took to the air. They were angry, they were noisy. Some hovered in the sky, others prowled around the cage. There was an atmosphere of menace coupled with an intelligence beyond our understanding. They held another convention; the crowd, now thousands strong, was in an ugly mood. I am sure they would have attacked anyone either brave or foolish enough to have ventured into either field that evening. Their protestations continued to nightfall and beyond.

Next morning there was no sign of any jackdaws except the decoy in the cage. It was dead but bore no mark of injury.

Humphrey Phelps 1974

# Cattle Trample a Fox

Sir,
Correspondence on the unusual behaviour of foxes prompts me to record the following incident which recently occurred on my farm. One morning, hearing the challenging notes of several

Red Polls and Herefords, our herdsman went towards a commotion where all the cows were milling round in a circle. In the middle of the circle was a young dog fox being trampled to death. Most of the cows had calves at foot, but the fox was familiar to them and had lived near their field for a year.

In addition, when the herdsman dragged the carcase away, he was charged heavily by two Red Poll matrons who are usually the most docile of his charges. The incident suggests the primitive instinct of herd protection and I wonder if it is known to be a common occurence against foxes.

Benjamin Ryecroft
*The Field*

## When a Fox Barked

When I was 14 years old I decided that I would like a cub for a pet. I went to the Dee estuary where I knew there was an earth. It was in a small rectangular field with a hedge bordering one side that was about 100 yards long. The earth was at the bottom of a dip. I managed to get a cub. But the beautiful bundle of fluff that used to sleep in my arms at night with nose tucked under my chin was by day a vicious, snarling demon.

Vicky was untameable. She would spring from my knees at anyone who approached me. She had to go. When I reached the long hedge near the earth from which I had taken her, I thought I saw a shadow of something passing at the side of me. I was about half-way down the hedge when a fox loped past and stopped 3 or 4 yards in front, looked at me and loped off again, setting up a series of soft barks, not the harsh yaps as they generally give.

Vicky's head shot up and trembled under my coat. Arriving at the dip I saw the vixen out with her other cubs. She and her mate were crouched on either side of the cubs and it was I who now trembled. I slid to my knees, slipping Vicky, who scampered to the others. The vixen quickly disappeared below with her cubs. I saw the fox watching me. He was standing upright. He lifted his nose with a full-throated bark.

More than 50 years have passed since this occurred. I have

wondered and pondered, but I have found no answer to all the questions that could be asked. Could the dog know that I was bringing back his cub? I shall never know.

Harold Taylor
*The Field*

# Horse Drowns Himself

The following is forwarded to us by Mr E. Eyre M.R.C.V.S., Penzance, Cornwall. – A curious case was brought under my notice some little time since of a horse that was living on a common, and doing no work, attempting to commit suicide by making his way into the sea, which was in close proximity, and deliberately backing into it and laying down to drown himself. He was, however, seen and, help being at hand, rescued. Some little time after he more than endeavoured to destroy himself by the same method, and this time he succeeded in effecting his purpose.

*The Veterinarian*, 1864

# Hearing-Power of a Horse

On two occasions the incredible happened with this horse – he ran away.

The first time was in the early morning when the boss had gone down as usual with the milk. The cart had been turned up the farm lane again with the empty cans, and Mr Boone was following hoeing off a weed or two, when all of a sudden Lightnin' threw up his shaggy head and burst into a tremendous gallop. So astonished was Mr Boone, he nearly dropped his hoe, and then began to run after him and shout. The runaway careered clumsily into the yard with a clatter of heavy wheels, a sparking of iron shoes, and a wild rattling of empty cans.

Brought hurriedly out of the house by the uproar, we found Lightnin' standing trembling against the shippon wall, which had barred his farther progress. The boss arrived in his clogs, panting.

'You silly beggar, what did you do that for?' he demanded grossly.

Lightnin' turned his long head, and seemed to blink, as if he were as much at a loss as the boss to account for his own undignified conduct.

'You silly beggar,' said the boss again, 'you're old enough to know better. What do you mean by leaving me behind like that?'

The horse appeared to shiver, as if ashamed of himself. But the affair was a mystery – there seemed to be no accounting for it.

In the evening we learned that at the identical moment that Lightnin' had broken into his gallop an express travelling at speed had crashed into a goods-train in a tunnel nearly two miles away. A number of persons had been killed. The old horse must have heard the impact, far too faint at that distance for the boss's ears.

Crichton Porteous
*Farmer's Creed* (1938)

# Adopted

A child of four years old, son of B. Burley, of Tregony, wandered away from his home the other day, when after some search, he was found under a sow, with a litter of young pigs, sucking away as busy as any of them. He had often made the pigs his playmates, but it was not known before that he had been so completely adopted into the family circle.

*The Bristol Journal*
25 April 1840

# The Old Sow

A woman named Charlotte Phinmore, the wife of a labourer resident in a place called Blackstone, has suckled a pig to her breast in order to rear it. She continued the practice in the presence of several witnesses and appeared to take as much care of it as if it had been a child. She was finally induced to desist by the interposition of several respectable persons. The neighbours have given the pig, which is about two weeks old, the name of Charlotte, while its nurse is known by the cognomen of the old sow. The pig and her infant have both been seen on her lap at the same time.

*The Plymouth Herald*
quoted in *The Falmouth Packet*, 20 August 1829

# Tea for the Parson, Beer for the Piggs

March 29th, 1777: Andrews the Smuggler brought me this night about 11 o'clock a bag of Hyson Tea 6Pd weight. He frightened us a little by whistling under the Parlour Window just as we were going to bed. I gave him some Geneva and paid him for the tea at 10/6 per Pd. 3. 3. 0.
April 15th, 1778: Brewed a vessell of strong Beer to-day. My two large Piggs by drinking some Beer grounds taking out of one of my Barrels to-day, got so amazingly drunk by it, that they were not able to stand and appeared like dead things almost, and so remained all night. I never saw Piggs so drunk in my life, I slit their ears for them without feeling.
April 16th, 1778: My 2 Piggs are still unable to walk yet, but they are better than they were yesterday. They tumble about yard and can by no means stand at all steady yet. In the afternoon my 2 Piggs were tolerably sober.

James Woodforde
*Diary of a Country Parson*

# Pig's Feast

On Monday last a party set out in a coach from Deal to spend the day in Waldershare Park, and instead of going to the Inn as most visitors do, they provided themselves with provisions, wines, spirits and porter, and when they alighted at the Park-gate, these refreshments were hid in a large amount of nettles, where it was supposed they would remain in safety. This, however, was not the case, for the party after taking a lounge in the Park found that some thieves, in the swinish shape, had arrived from the adjoining Farm-yard, and had devoured the whole of the eatables, and having broken the bottles, had drunk the liquors, etc., and were ranging about in a state of intoxication; the looker in the Park was alarmed at the appearance of the animals and suspecting that they were seized with a complaint called the staggerbone, he immediately sent to Eythorne for a farrier, before whose arrival, however, the cause of their extraordinary appearance was discovered. The chagrin of the party at the loss of their refreshments may be more easily conceived than expressed.

*Kentish Chronicle*
25 July 1817

# A Warning to Drunkards

Last week Mr Castle, farmer, of Northbourne, while brewing some strong ale, left a portion of it in what is called the well-lodge, to cool, when one of the cows got from the farmyard into the place, and drank so plentifully of the potent beverage that she was shortly taken ill; a farrier was sent for who administered the proper remedies, but to no effect, for in a few hours the poor animal actually died in a state of intoxication, a warning to drunkards.

*Kent Chronicle*
14 April 1838

# My Friend the Pig

One morning as I passed the pen he (my friend the pig) grunted – spoke, I may say – in such a pleasant friendly way that I had to stop and return his greeting; then, taking an apple from my pocket, I placed it in his trough. He turned it over with his snout, then looked up and said something like 'Thank-you' in a series of gentle grunts. Then he bit off and ate a small piece, then another small bite, and eventually taken what was left in his mouth he finished eating it. After that he always expected me to stay a minute and speak to him when I went to the field; I knew it from his way of greeting me, and on such occasions I gave him an apple. But he never ate it greedily: he appeared more inclined to talk than to eat, until by degrees I came to understand what he was saying. What he said was that he appreciated my kind intentions in giving him apples. But, he went on, to tell the real truth, it is not a fruit I am particularly fond of. I am familiar with its taste as they sometimes give me apples, usually the small unripe or bad ones that fall from the trees. However, I don't actually dislike them. I get skim milk and am rather fond of it; then a bucket of mash, which is good enough for hunger; but what I enjoy most is a cabbage, only I don't get one very often now. I sometimes think that if they would let me out of this muddy pen to ramble like the sheep and other beasts of the field or on the downs I should be able to pick up a number of morsels which would taste better than anything they give me. Apart from the subject of food, I hope you won't mind my telling you that I'm rather fond of being scratched on the back.

So I scratched him vigorously with my stick, and made him wriggle his body and wink and blink and smile delightedly all over his face, Then I said to myself: 'Now what the juice can I do more to please him?' For though under sentence of death, he had done no wrong, but was a good, honest-hearted fellow-mortal, so that I felt bound to do something to make the mirey remnant of his existence a little less miserable.

I think it was the word juice I had just used – for that was how I pronounced it to make it less like a swear-word – that gave me an inspiration. In the garden, a few yards back from the pen, there was a large clump of old elder-trees, now over-loaded with ripening fruit – the biggest clusters I had ever seen. Going to the trees I selected and cut the finest bunch I could find, as big round as my cap, and weighing over a pound. This I deposited in his trough and invited him to try it. He sniffed at it a little doubtfully, and looked at me and made a remark or two, then nibbled at the edge of the cluster, taking a few berries into his mouth, and holding them some time before he ventured to crush them, At length he did venture, then looked at me again and made more remarks. 'Queer fruit this! Never tasted anything quite like it before, but I really can't say yet whether I like it or not.'

Then he took another bite, then more bites, looking up at me, and saying something between the bites, till, little by little, he had consumed the whole bunch; then turning round, he went back to his bed with a little grunt to say that I was now at liberty to go on to the cows and horses.

However, on the following morning he hailed my approach in such a lively manner, with such a note of expectancy in his voice, that I concluded he had been thinking a great deal about elder-berries, and was anxious to have another go at them. Accordingly I cut him another bunch, while he quickly consumed, making little exclamations the while – 'Thank you, thank you, very good – very good indeed!' It was a new sensation in his life, and made him very happy, and was almost as good as a day of liberty in the fields and meadows and on the open green downs.

From that time I visited him two or three times a day to give him huge clusters of elder-berries. There were plenty for the starlings as well; the clusters on those trees would have filled a cart.

Then one morning I heard an indignant scream from the garden and peeping out saw my friend the pig, bound hand and foot, being lifted by a dealer into his cart with the assistance of the farmer.

'Good-bye, old boy!' said I as the cart drove off; and I thought that by and by, in a month or two, if several persons discovered a peculiar and fascinating flavour in their morning rasher, it would be due to the elderberries I had supplied to my friend the pig, which had gladdened his heart for a week or two before receiving his quietus.

W.H. Hudson
*The Book of a Naturalist* (1919)

# Going Home

A gentleman residing at Caversham bought two pigs at Reading market, which were conveyed to his house in a sack, and turned into his yard, which lies on the banks of the river Thames. The next morning the pigs were missing; a hue and cry was immediately raised, and towards the afternoon a person gave information that two pigs had been seen swimming across the river at nearly its broadest part. They were afterwards observed trotting along the Pangbourn road; and in one place where the road branches off, putting their noses together, as if in deep consultation; the result was their safe return to the place from which they were originally conveyed to Reading, a distance of nine miles and by cross roads. The farmer from whom they had been purchased, brought them back to their owner, but they took the very first opportunity to escape, recrossed the water like two dogs (thus removing the stigma on their race, which proverbially disqualifies them for swimming without cutting their own throats) and never stopped until they found themselves at their first home.

In this instance we see difficulties overcome, and an element encountered to which the animals could not have been accustomed, in order to arrive at a far distant place to which they were attached. It is evident that the recollection of that place, and of their early associates, influenced the proceedings of the animals; but that they should be in possession of a faculty which induced them to swim a river, and led them in an almost direct line to their distant home, is not a little to be wondered at.

Edward Jesse
*Gleanings in Natural History*, Volume II, 1838

# A Sagacious Dog

Mr. Knight, the principal landed proprietor at Isleham, in Suffolk, preserved the game on the manor of which he was lord. One day he saw a man, with his dog, hunting in the open field for game; who, as soon as he saw him, made off, being at a considerable distance when he was first discovered, and Mr Knight found it would be useless to pursue him. He heard, however, a shrill whistle, and immediately saw the dog fall down. He rode up to him, and found him apparently dead, being stretched out at length, his eyes closed, and, to all appearance, breathless. Mr. Knight whipped the dog severely, and endeavoured to make his horse tread upon him, but all to no purpose. The animal was immovable, and seemed to be quite inanimate. Mr. Knight therefore left him, half persuaded that he was dead. He kept his eye, however, upon the spot, and when he had got to a considerable distance, he saw the dog rise, look cautiously about him, and, when he found the coast clear, he set off full speed after his master.

Edward Jesse
*Gleanings in Natural History*, Volume II, 1838

# Cat and Dog

'You'd think that cat was the new landlord at the Vine,' I said, 'the way it owns the place.'

'Has Chris told you about him and the Labrador?'

'Not yet,' I said.

'Chris had that cat for years, and the two of them was that close that Chris could hardly draw a pint of beer without the cat on his shoulder. Daft, we used to say, and Chris would laugh, and you'd swear the cat was laughing too. Then someone gave Chris a dog, a Labrador, a fine black Labrador, and the cat went mad jealous, spitting and snarling and ready with its claws at every moment of the day. "You'll have to get rid of one of them," we used to tell him. Well, you'd be scared to sit in the bar with that cat if the dog showed his nose at the window or the door. And so it went on all winter. "You'll lose trade," we said to Chris; "people don't like cats spitting in their beer," we said.

'And then one night, end of January when the floods was up, just before closing time Chris puts the cat outside the door for a few minutes same as he always did at that time. Such a night – as bad as I ever remember and the house like an island with the floods. Well, he was hardly back behind the bar to serve us a last round when we heard a screech that would frighten you – a badger's screech it was, and a minute later there was another. Did you ever hear a badger screech? Like six cats only louder. So Chris rushes out to see what's happened and the wind bangs the door and we all sits there waiting for him to come back. And then he comes in with the cat in his arms, flat out the animal was – dead, we thought. And Mrs Chris sits down and takes it on her lap, and there was a lump on its head like a hen's egg, and its coat was torn and thick with mud. No, it wasn't bitten, badgers only fight with their claws. And when anybody touched it, it shivered – proper hurt it was. And then in comes the big Labrador from the kitchen, and it goes up to the cat and it starts licking it – licks it all over, and presently the cat opens its eyes and sees the dog, and it never moves. And the dog goes on licking and licking, kind of comforting. And do you know from that instant moment those two animals was friends – bosom friends, you might call 'em. They'd sleep together o' nights, and if in the daytime the dog was shut inside the kennel the cat would climb up and lie on top of the wire just to be near him.

Robert Gibbings
*Till I End My Song* (1957)

# Saved by a Rat

Mr Ferryman also communicated to me the following anecdote of a rat, which I am in justice to him bound to admit he did not implicitly believe himself, neither are my readers required to do so: I merely give the story as I heard it. He said that he had an old friend, a clergyman, of retired and studious habits. When sitting in his room one day, he saw an English rat come out of a hole at the bottom of the wainscot; he threw it a piece of bread, and in process of time he so familiarized the animal that it became perfectly tame, ran about him, was his constant companion, and appeared much attached to him. He was in the habit of reading in bed at night; and was on one occasion awoke by feeling a sharp bite on his cheek, when he discovered the curtains of his bed to be on fire. He made his escape, but his house was burnt down, and he saw no more of his rat. He was however convinced, and remained so for the rest of his life, that his old companion had saved him from being burnt to death by biting his cheek, and thus making him aware of his danger. The marks of teeth were visible upon it, and the reader may put what faith he pleases on the supposition of the good clergyman. He himself was always indignant if anyone doubted it.

Edward Jesse
*Gleanings in Natural History*, Volume II, 1838

# Chicknapper

In the poultry yard to-day there is a striking example of philosophy. A sermon, not in stone but in a pot egg. Apparently one can learn, even from a hen, something of the art of cutting one's losses. One of mine was persistently broody. She sat herself in the hen house and nothing would discourage her. All the eggs were removed, so she sat upon a pot one, tirelessly, endlessly, until her feathers grew ragged, her eye wild, and she herself got thinner and thinner, consumed with the maternal instinct. I was lazy about shutting her up, thinking she would get sick of it. After five weeks she did. She arose, spurned the pot egg, that poor and disappointing thing which after endless days of cherishing in her bosom remained in unbroken chilliness. She marched forth into the world and found another hen, growing slightly weary of a six weeks' brood. To them she addressed herself, clucked and scratched and offered larger and fluffier wings than their rightful parent, who after a few futile efforts to dislodge the interloper, abandoned them. The triumph of the 'go-getter' was complete and she proudly parades with a company of decidedly oversize chickens.

Lilias Rider Haggard
*A Norfolk Notebook* (1946)

# Send for the Vet

The veterinary lecturer at Cirencester College told me that during the cattle plague in the sixties [1860s] he had a coat well worth £50 to any veterinary surgeon, so impregnated was it with the infection. This man was fond of scoring off the students, and had a habit at the commencement of each lecture of holding a short viva voce examination on the subject of the last. I remember when the tables were turned on him by a ready-witted student. The lecturer, who was a superior veterinary surgeon, detailed a whole catalogue of exaggerated symptoms exhibited by an imaginary horse, and selecting his victim added, with a chuckle, 'Now, Mr K., perhaps you will kindly tell us what treatment you would adopt under these circumstances?' K. was not a very diligent student, and the lecturer expected a display of ignorance, but his anticipated triumph was cut short by the reply, 'Well, if I had a horse as bad as all that I should send for the vet.' The lecturer expostulated, but could get nothing further out of K., and was forced to recognise that the general laugh which followed was against himself.

A.H. Savory
*Grain and Chaff from an English Manor* (Blackwell, 1920)

# Rat-Catcher

Cecil Chapman was renowned for rat-catching. We would go with him when the threshing-tackle was busy at farms. Like ships' rats, stack rats always try to leave a sinking stack as soon as they become aware of what is happening. We would take forked sticks – holding them down for the terriers, or to give them quietus with a steel-tipped heel of our clodhoppers.

Not so Cecil Chapman. With a big red hand he would snatch a rat from the rick, take it to his mouth and, with a quick snap of sharp incisors behind the rat's ears, he would sever the spinal vertibrae. With his killings there was never a squeak or a wriggle. And despite these unorthodox and unhygienic activities, Cecil was never ill.

Spike Mays
*Reuben's Corner* (1969)

# A Warning to Stockmen

Towards daybreak the mare Scot foaled, a 'fine upstanding foal,' as they say here. This morning I found Fairhead rolling the new pasture, No.10, in the heavy rain. One of the oldest and quietest horses on the farm was dragging the wooden roller, but when it saw me advancing upon it beneath an umbrella it took fright, and nearly precipitated itself and the roller into the ditch. Sensible as they are, farm-horses draw the line at umbrellas, to which they are unaccustomed. When we had finished the rolling, I went with Fairhead to see the foal. Undoing the door of the box, he entered it, still wearing his wet military greatcoat; whereupon the mare, although he called out at her, laid back her ears and drew back her lips. Indeed, she looked, very nasty, and I thought that she meant to attack him, an opinion which Fairhead shared, for he got out of the box as quickly as he could. Remarking that he had never known her behave like this before, he tried to re-enter, with the same result. Then the solution of the mystery struck him.

'She don't know me in this here coat,' he said, 'and can't smell me through it': and, pulling it off, he went into the box boldly. The mare thrust out her head and sniffed, then she literally seemed 'to smile all over', as the Americans say, and made no further attempt to interfere with him, even when he caught hold of the foal and dragged it on to its legs. Two or three years ago a change of the stockman's clothes resulted in a tragedy in this neighbourhood. My friend Mr. Henry Smith, the squire of Ellingham, had a bailiff named Bensely. Also he had a very savage bull. The bull was turned out on a marsh, where it could injure no one, but Bensely, unhappily for himself, went to look at it after church or chapel, dressed in his Sunday best. The bull did not know its attendant in his attire, and attacked him so that the poor man was found dead in a dyke.

H. Rider Haggard
*A Farmer's Year* (1898)

# Shepherd and Dog

It was on Honister Pass. I was walking among the rough quarry-rubbish, some distance above the road, looking for pretty stones. In the great silence of the place there was a murmur from the beck below, hardly noticeable. The tops of the steep ridges on either side of the dale were lost in this cloud. All at once the silence was broken by a most musical voice from nowhere. Lost in cloud, a shepherd was calling. Soon he came into sight on the opposite hill, called again, and was answered from above my head. The second shepherd seemed to stand perpendicularly above me, a thousand feet or so away; he looked tiny, on his headland of crag. Between him and me his dog was working. I had not noticed any sheep; but now I saw them, in the most impossible situations. The dog had to coax them down from green ledges on crag-faces, ledges which looked as narrow as a fox's bink. He was a discreet dog; he made no sudden movement and gave no sign of urgency, as long as the sheep was in a dangerous place. He approached quietly, so that the sheep might move off, wary but not alarmed, just as quietly. When it reached safe ground, he allowed himself to hustle it a little, down towards the road, where quite a flock had surprisingly assembled from nowhere.

He thought he had finished his task, and mounted guard a little way above the assembled flock; the shepherd and dog on the other side of the valley were coming down beside the sheep they had gathered. But the man whom I saw standing a thousand feet above me was still there, searching the heights, and all at once he called his dog by a series of whistles, and off bounded the dog, not to his master, but to the point to which his master had mysteriously told him to go. The most venturous sheep of all had been detected perching suicidally on a crag-face, and why it ever went there, heaven knew; and how the dog was to get it away safely, perhaps the dog knew.

He did. He went to the foot of the crag and barked angrily. The sheep made a scared scramble upwards – the only direction in which it had any foothold. The impetus of the rush carried the creature to the green brow of the crag, and safety. If the dog had approached any other way, the sheep would have dashed down to destruction: and if the dog had not put some fierceness into his voice, the sheep might have been there yet. It was a masterpiece of judgment, and it took place at least six hundred yards away from the shepherd, who gave no guidance but a few whistles and a melodious tenor call.

Doreen Wallace
*English Lakeland* (1948)

## Geese

Mr Studdy (loftily persistent): 'A goose is same as a cow; they both want a nice bite o' grass an' plenty o' clean water. Leastaways, English geese do; I don't know nawthen about furrin birds. Never had no truck wi' sech, an' I don't want I should, t'ain't likely.'

The Scribe (emphatically as he points to the Toulouse gander and geese on Mr Studdy's pasture): 'They're from Toulouse, and Toulouse is in the south of France.'

Mr Studdy (very annoyed): 'That don't sinify nothin' to me where Toulouse is. Them geese is as English as I am an' if anybody towd me they ain't, I'd call him a liar, beggin' y'r pardon.'

The Scribe (indifferently): 'They don't lay nearly so well as Chinese geese.'

Mr Studdy (coldly): 'I don't want they should. They lay well enough f'r th' likes o' me. (Passionately): I ouldn't have a Chiny goose on my meddy if somebody bin an' pide me to put it there. I do wholly wonder th' p'liceman ain't been on to ye about 'em. (Confusedly): Taking a livin' outer honest men's mouths along of a lot of furriners.'

S.L. Bensusan
*Back of Beyond* (1945)

## Pheasant versus Bishop

One Sunday afternoon I was returning from a walk on the Quantocks down Triscombe Combe. My Cairn terrier was ranging through the bracken out on the hill in the hope of finding a rabbit to chase. At intervals I gave my peculiar whistle to indicate my position.

Out from the bracken beside me came a magnificent cock pheasant minus his tail. He fell in alongside of me and we walked along together. He changed his position at intervals, tacking successively to the right and left of me. I told him I appreciated his company and remarked admiringly on his splendid appearance, also condoling the loss of his tail. It soon became apparent that he was far from appreciating my kind words. He showed signs of rising wrath and indignation, making rude noises in his throat and, ruffling out his neck feathers, his eyes filled with bile and ire. I continued to speak the kindly word which is alleged to turn away wrath but to no avail. His rage and fury rose in crescendo and he proceeded to attack my stick, giving it a couple of strong pecks.

Next, he tried to get at my shins and I spent some minutes exercising my wrists in the fencer's art of parrying gently but firmly his repeated attacks. He then forged ahead, turned to face me again and assumed the crouching attitude which pheasants adopt when about to fly. My face was in his direct line as target and I was constrained to fetch him a sharp but not lethal tap on his head.

It was not a bad shot with my stick for one with only one eye and it laid him out. My problem was what to do next. Should I finish him off and carry him to the keeper's cottage, or to my neighbour who rears pheasants? There was a long way to go.

I wondered how I could explain to anyone I met, the appearance of a bishop, and dressed as such, carrying a fine pheasant and that on a good Sunday afternoon. To say I had been attacked by the bird and had had to kill it would have taxed credulity and cast doubts about episcopal goings-on and veracity. As I cogitated the bird began to come round. It waved its legs, flapped its wings and opened an eye, still full of bile. I decided to leave him to return whence he came and hoped I had taught him some manners. As I went on my way I kept turning to see what he was doing. My last view was of a bleary pheasant pursuing a drunken course back to the bracken.

I pondered on the reason for this attack. At first I thought that losing his tail might have embittered him against all living things and who more appropriate than a bishop to be the recipient of abuse? Then a more likely explanation occurred to me. As mentioned, my neighbour rears pheasants and when he feeds them whistles to bid them 'come to the cookhouse door, boys'. I had been whistling to Susie, my Cairn, so the bird must have heard me and thought the bar was open. Finding only kind words and neither meat nor drink, he felt cheated and enraged. I have not seen him again, so presumably he has since satisfied someone else's appetite.

Maurice H. Harland
*The Field*

# Cormorant and Herons

Looking down from my bedroom window on to a salmon pool 150 feet below, I noticed the arrival of a cormorant in the tail of the pool, which immediately began the usual series of upstream dives.

During the first dive a heron arrived on the bank, in line with the spot where the cormorant submerged, and started running along the bank as if to keep pace with him.

During each of the first four dives the heron jumped into the water 18 inches below the bank, his beak and feet arriving almost simultaneously, and each time secured and ate a fish, then ran on to catch up with the cormorant between meals.

The heron then flew away and was immediately replaced by another. At this moment the cormorant dived for the fifth time right through the salmon lie, and surfaced above a submerged sandbank near the opposite side of the river with a clam, 6 inches long, in his beak.

He broke up the clam in about a minute, ate it, and then flew away, as did the second and disappointed heron. The salmon continued to show freely all down the pool during the whole operation, when they could not have failed to have seen the cormorant.

Later the same day two other fishermen co-operated. I hooked a big fish through the dorsal fin with a tube-fly. He was running and got badly snagged. My neighbour on the other bank cast his line across mine, freed the fish, which he played and landed for me.

R.W. Corbett
*The Field*

# Showers of Aphids

At about three o'clock in the afternoon of that day, which was very hot, the people of this village were surprised by a shower of aphides, or smother-flies, which fell in these parts. Those that were walking in the street at that juncture found themselves covered with these insects, which settled also on the hedges and gardens, blackening all the vegetables where they alighted. My annuals were discoloured with them, and the stalks of a bed of onions were quite coated over for six days after. These armies, were then, no doubt, in a state of emigration, and shifting their quarters: and might have come, as we know, from the great hop plantations of Kent or Sussex, the wind being all that day in the easterly quarter. They were observed, at the same time, in great clouds, about Farnham, and all along the vale from Farnham to Alton.

Gilbert White
*Natural History of Selbourne* (1789)

# Worms

Worms do not possess any sense of hearing. They took not the least notice of the shrill notes from a metal whistle, which was repeatedly sounded near them; nor did they of the deepest and loudest tones of a bassoon. They were indifferent to shouts, if care was taken that the breath did not strike them. When placed on a table close to the keys of a piano, which was played as loudly as possible, they remained perfectly quiet.

Although they were indifferent to undulations in the air

audible by us, they are extremely sensitive to vibrations in any solid object. When the pots containing two worms which had remained quite indifferent to the sound of the piano, were placed on this instrument, and the note C in the bass clef was struck, both instantly retreated to their burrows. After a time they emerged, and when G above the line in the treble clef was struck they again retreated. Under similar circumstances on another night one worm dashed into its burrow on a very high note being struck only once, and the other worm when C in the treble clef was struck. On these occasions the worms were not touching the sides of the pots, which stood in saucers; so that the vibrations, before reaching their bodies, had to pass from the sounding board of the piano, through the saucer, the bottom of the pot and the damp, not very compact earth on which they lay with their tails in their burrows. They often showed their sensitiveness when the pot in which they lived, or the table on which the pot stood, was accidentally and lightly struck; but they appeared less sensitive to such jars than to the vibrations of the piano; and their sensitiveness to jars varied much at different times.

It has often been said that if the ground is beaten or otherwise made to tremble, worms believe that they are pursued by a mole and leave their burrows. From one account that I have received, I have no doubt that this is often the case; but a gentleman informs me that he lately saw eight or ten worms leave their burrows and crawl about the grass on some boggy land on which two men had just trampled while setting a trap; and this appeared in a part of Ireland where there were no moles. I have been assured by a Volunteer that he has often seen many large earth-worms crawling quickly about the grass, a few minutes after his company had fired a volley with blank cartridges. The peewit (Tringa vanellus, Linn.) seems to know instinctively that worms will emerge if the ground is made to tremble; for Bishop Stanley states (as I hear from Mr Moorhouse) that a young peewit kept in confinement used to stand on one leg and beat the turf with the other leg until the worms crawled out of their burrows, when they were instantly devoured.

Charles Darwin
*Vegetable Mould And Earthworms* (1881)

# A Swallow's Nest

A certain swallow built, for two years together, on the handles of a pair of garden shears, that were stuck up against the walls in an outhouse, and therefore must have her nest spoiled whenever that implement was wanted. And, what is stranger still, another bird of the same species built its nest on the wings and body of an owl, that happened by accident to hang dead and dry from the rafter of a barn. This owl, with the nest on its wings, and with eggs in the nest, was brought as a curiosity worthy the most elegant private museum in Great Britain. The owner, struck with the oddity of the sight, furnished the bringer with a large shell, or conch, desiring him to fix it just where the owl hung. The person did as he was ordered; and the following year, a pair, probably the same pair, built their nest in the conch, and laid their eggs.

The owl and the conch made a strange, grotesque appearance, and are not the least curious specimens in that wonderful collection of art and nature.

Thus is instinct in animals, taken the least out of its way, an undistinguishing, limited faculty, and blind to every circumstance that does not immediately respect self-preservation, or lead at once to the propagation or support of their species.

Gilbert White
*Natural History of Selbourne* (1789)

# Jackdaw Nests

And here will be the properest place to mention, while I think of it, an anecdote which the above-mentioned gentleman told me when I was last at his house; which was, that in a warren joining to his outlet, many daws (corvi Monedulae) build every year in the rabbit-burrows under ground. The way he and his brothers used to take their nests, while they were boys, was by listening at the mouths of the holes, and if they heard the young ones cry, they twisted the nests out with a forked stick. Some water-fowls (viz. the puffins) breed, I know, in this manner; but I should never have suspected the daws of building in holes on the flat ground.

Another very unlikely spot is made use of by daws as a place to breed in, and that is Stonehenge. These birds deposit their nests in the interstices between the upright and the impost stones of the amazing work of antiquity; which circumstance alone speaks the prodigious height of the upright stones, that they should be tall enough to secure those nests from the annoyance of shepherd boys, who are always idling round the place.

Gilbert White
*Natural History of Selbourne* (1789)

# The Nightingale, Essex

I never heard a nightingale in better voice, nor do I remember one singing so close to my door. All the garden throbbed with music and I was beginning to think I found in it some of the magic that was there for Keats, when, suddenly, the bombers came. Scores of them roaring close overhead and others following in quick succession as the earlier flights faded out in the distance. In the quieter intervals I still strained to hear the nightingale; it sang on unperturbed and I heard for a time the perfect symbol of the world at war – the song of the nightingale faintly audible under the deadly drumming of the bombers. When the nightingale flew on to a more distant tree it was not the noise that disturbed her, but my friendly shadow trying to creep a little closer.

Kingsley Martin, 12 August 1944
*Critic's London Diary* (1960)

# Paupers and Vagabonds

# Death of a Poor Man

One night when I called to see him, coming home from work, he burst into tears. 'Tha be gwoin' to take ma away, an I dwun want to go,' he cried. I tried to comfort him, as well as I was able, but all to no purpose; he was beside himself with grief. And was it any wonder? Would you like to have gone, if you had been in his place? After living within those old walls, hallowed with memories of his mother and dad, his childhood and many things beside, for nearly eighty years, working and slaving and sweating and stinting, for what? for what? But I have told you already. Of course he did not want to go; and quite right too. He was natural and manly, honest and brave; it is only the coward that thinks otherwise; and the spirit should be commended, not blamed and stifled down, and quenched out of existence. Several times the officers called and asked him if he would go to the 'house', but each time he answered defiantly, 'No, I wunt.' The old man shrank into the bed-clothes, and peered out at them over the top of the sheet. 'I'd soonder starve, an' die in mi bed fust, than go to that place,' he protested. Then the officers went away. The next day a conveyance stopped before the cottage, in came the officer again, and two men to carry him off. At first the old man wept like a child, then bawled and shouted at the interlopers: 'Leave ma alwun.' 'I wunt go.' 'Le ma die in me bed.' 'Get a hatchet an chop mi 'ed off'; but all to no purpose. They dragged him out of bed, pulled a pair of woollen stockings on his shrunken shanks, clapped a blanket and an old coat around him, hauled him out of the cottage, slipped him in the conveyance, banged the door and drove off as hard as they were able.

He did not live many weeks at the workhouse.

Alfred Williams
*A Wiltshire Village* (1912)

# The Beggars

On Thursday, May 27th [1800], a very tall woman, tall much beyond the measure of tall women, called at the door. She had on a very long brown cloak, and a very white cap without Bonnet – her face was excessively brown, but it had plainly once been fair. She led a little bare-footed child about 2 years old by the hand and said her husband who was a tinker had gone before with the other children. I gave her a piece of Bread. Afterwards on my road to Ambleside, beside the Bridge at Rydale, I saw her husband sitting by the roadside, his two asses feeding beside him and the two young children at play upon the grass. The man did not beg. I passed on and about a 1/4 of a mile further I saw two boys before me, one about 10 the other about 8 years old at play chasing a butterfly. They were wild figures, not very ragged, but without a shoes and stockings; the hat of the elder was wreathed round with yellow flowers, the younger whose hat was only a rimless crown, had stuck it round with laurel leaves. They continued at play till I drew very near and then they addressed me with the Beggars' cant and the whining voice of sorrow. I said I served your mother this morning. (The Boys were so like the woman who had called at the door that I could not be mistaken.) O! says the elder you could not serve my mother for she's dead and my father's on at the next town – he's a potter. I persisted in my assertion and that I would give them nothing. Says the elder Come, let's away, and away they flew like lightning. They had however sauntered so long in their road that they did not reach Ambleside before me, and I saw them go up to Matthew Harrison's house with their wallet upon the elder's shoulder, and creeping with a Beggar's complaining foot. On my return through Ambleside I met in the street the mother driving her asses; in the two Panniers of one of which were the two little children whom she was chiding and threatening with a wand which she used to drive on her asses, while the little things hung in wantonness over the Pannier's edge.

Dorothy Wordsworth
*Journals*

# Turk Taylor

In this parish dwells a vacuous but amiable old fellow called Turk
Taylor, who has no belongings and picks up a living heaven
knows how, for beyond a parish cottage which he occupies, and
some small allowance from the rates, supplemented by an
occasional job of pig-herding, he has no visible means of
subsistence. Five or six years ago, in the course of a very hard
winter, I heard that poor Turk Taylor had been found lying on the
floor of his cottage at death's door from cold and starvation. He
was attended to and his wants relieved, and afterwards an attempt
was made to remove him to the workhouse. If I remember rightly
the relieving officer actually came to fetch him, but the poor old
man, getting wind of his designs, hid himself in a ditch until that
official had departed, with the result that he still continues his
free but precarious existence.

H. Rider Haggard
*A Farmer's Year* (Longmans, 1899)

# Not So Deficient

The J.P. examining mental powers of alleged mental deficient in
a rural poor law institution, asked: 'Now, my girl, if you had a
pound and bought 5s. worth of groceries, how much would you
have left?' No answer. Finally, the master intervened and urged
Jane to give her answer. Jane, with an offended air: 'If this old
fool doesn't know, I'm not going to tell him.'
    J.P., delighted, 'She's all right.'

*The Countryman Book* (1948)

# The Old Doctor

Dr F—, during the first decade of the 20th century, was a
general practitioner and the medical officer to the village Union

or Poor Law Institution. He was a man who enjoyed a day's shooting and several glasses of whisky daily.

On his regular visits to the Union, a comparative newcomer to that establishment always asked to have his chest examined. Eventually Dr. F— said to him, 'Now, look here, my man, every time I come here you ask me to examine your chest and each time I've examined it and told you that there's nothing wrong with your chest. So why do you want me to examine it over and over again?'

'Oh, that's easy, doctor,' replied the old man. 'It's like this here, before I came into this place I used to get a drop of whisky now and again. Now, I don't get none, but the smell of your breath is lovely.'

After a day's shooting one Boxing Day, Dr. F— was sitting down to dinner in his host's farmhouse when a message came for the doctor to go to the Union immediately. On arrival the doctor found that an old man had tried to cut his throat. After attending to the old man's throat, Dr. F— admonished his patient. 'Now, look here, my man, don't you ever try this job again when I've had a tiring day's shooting and am just about to eat a good hot dinner.'

Then in a more kindly tone, the Doctor continued, 'However, if you should ever feel inclined to cut your throat again, do it at a more reasonable time. And for goodness sake cut it across not up and down like you've just done.'

'Yes, doctor,' said the old man, 'but, you see, I did the best I could in the dark.'

Humphrey Phelps

## Extract from the Rules, Orders and Objects of the Herefordshire Agricultural Society founded in 1797

5. To reward labourers who shall bring up, or have already brought up the greatest number of legitimate children, without any or with the smallest relief from their respective parishes.

Arthur Young
*Annals of Agriculture* (*c.* 1797)

# A Gypsy Fight

I was helping George tidy up his bakehouse when I heard a lumbering of wheels out in the Street and a trampling of many horses. I ran down the yard to see. Caravan after caravan came past, some as bright and polished as new pins and some as shaky at the axle it was a wonder they did not fall to pieces in the road. They were gipsies moving on from some farm where they had recently been paid off. The men sat at the doors of the caravans, with the reins hanging over their wrists. They looked relaxed and sleepy and yet ready like an animal to spring suddenly into action. In straggling knots the women walked behind, dirty and glamorous; and the hum of their deep voices, as they talked among themselves, rang through my head like a bell. Barefooted children padded along, boys with both hands thrust into their pockets, spitting like grown-ups, and girls in pitiful rags. The procession was so long that soon George too had come out to see what was happening. He stood at my side now, scornful but interested.

'That's a queer lingo they're talking. Listen!' he said.

It was not words I was listening to, however, but a music that had me in thrall.

'Why, bless me,' George was saying, 'if there isn't another gang of 'em coming the other way, now! Is it a gathering of the clans, or what?'

And then I saw a second procession of caravans turning the corner from the opposite direction. From the leader of each party the word was passed down the line to halt, and the men slipped from their seats, flung the reins over the horses' backs, and hurried up to the front. Soon all the villagers were at their doors, watching. For a while the gipsies stood about in the roadway, talking, alert now and bright-eyed in greeting. Then, when somebody had been put in charge of each caravan, they disappeared into the Forsyth Arms.

It was from the owner of this pub that we afterwards learned something of what happened next; but it did not amount to much, for the gipsies mostly spoke in their own tongue. As George had unwittingly suggested, this was a meeting of the clans. Long ago these two divisions of the same tribe had apparently split and gone their separate ways, divided for all time, as they supposed, by a riving feud. Now, unexpectedly, they had met, who hoped never to meet again – as two severed friends might suddenly find themselves face to face in a foreign land. Gipsy blood binds fast; and in the flush of first meeting it had been agreed to forget old differences, however deep, and drink together in amity again. For a long while all went well – for so long, in fact, that Fladmere grew tired of staring at the lines of empty caravans and went back to its work, thinking the drama over. But it had hardly begun. The next we all knew was that the Street had suddenly become a battlefield. Drink had burned away the gipsies' better feelings. Old angers were rekindled. At first the men were content to bring their glasses out into the road, and carry on their argument there; but soon they flung the drinks away, tore off their coats, and began fighting. Fiercely they grappled, until their shirts were shredded from their backs. I could hear the thud of blows where I stood trembling at the gate before I was hurried indoors out of the way. At the first opportunity I fled upstairs to the favourite showroom window and stood watching the battle from there. It had ceased to be a series of isolated fights now and had become a ranging of side against side, clan against clan.

I think such a battle was fought that day in Fladmere as must have given the village a lasting memorial in the annals of those fiery people. Bare to the waist the men pitched into one another, rolling their clenched bodies on the granite heaps by the roadside. I could see the blood streaming down their naked bodies. The women stood by screaming their encouragement. But these were Amazons, and soon they too had joined actively in the fight. They hurled lumps of stone at one another, yelling as they did so. They grappled like the men, clawing and tearing out one another's hair. The Street was full of the snarling and screaming of the gipsies. Cottagers hurried out and secured their garden gates; and while George bolted the yardway doors, somebody else flung up the shutters in front of the shop. In the excitement I must have been forgotten, for I stood undisturbed at the showroom window for some time. Right underneath me the fighters pressed, so that I could see how matted with blood was their hair and hear the swinging blows. My knees shook, and every now and then I would run to the back of the room and and hide myself in the shadows; but soon my feverish curiosity drove me to the window again, as the cries increased in the road below. Nausea filled the pit of my stomach, but I would not let myself be sick. Then somebody came and dragged me away. If I was scolded I do not remember, for I did not even hear what was being said to me. I only knew that for the remainder of the day every wagon that passed made me think I was hearing the rumble of approaching caravans, and at every raised voice in the Street my heart beat quicker for fear it should be the gipsies returning.

C. Henry Warren
*A Boy in Kent* (1937)

# Gypsy Cure

The Smiths also told me much medical lore of the Gypsies, the most memorable account being that of their curing of their seventh child Loowey, when she was dying of pneumonia. The gawje* doctor had told the parents that he could do no more for the child and that they must be prepared to lose her during the night. White Will and his fellow Gypsies then decided to take over, and to use the Romany cure of the plastering of the lungs with warm cow dung. The treatment necessitated the covering of the lung areas with warm dung, both front and back of the body, renewing the plaster as soon as it lost its warmth and thus its drawing powers. To have the plaster at its very best the dung should be obtained fresh from the cow. Thus through one afternoon and a whole night the Gypsies chased a herd of cows around the fields in the obtaining of warm dung from them. And when the doctor arrived on the next day, the child, whom he had expected to find dying or dead, was sitting upright on her mother's lap supping bread and milk. The treatment was then continued in modified form, the dung being obtained in a more simple way from the cow pats in the fields, and heated in tin cans over the fire. The child made a speedy and full recovery from pneumonia. The doctor carefully took down into his note-book all details of the cure – 'for future use', he declared.

Juliette de Bairacli Levy
*As Gypsies Wander* (1953)

*Non-Gypsy

# Church and Chapel

# Opposition

The people of the pretty little Cotswold village of Lower Guiting don't go to church, and, what is more to the point, they declare that they won't. The letters that have appeared in our columns during the past two months supply the reason for such a determined attitude, i.e. opposition to the vicar (Rev. J.E. Green) and his alleged ritualistic innovations in the church service.

On Monday was reported the arrival of the Bishop Hooper van in the village. The van belongs to the Church Association and National Protestant League, the aim of which is expressed in large characters upon the van as 'the maintenance of the Protestant character of the Church of England.' It professes to do this by sending lecturers into the parishes, in town and country, where ritualism is said to be rampant, to stir up the parishioners against 'the introduction into the Church of England of the abominable practices of ritualism, confession and absolution of the Church of Rome' as the lecturers call it. On Monday the Bishop Hooper van journeyed from Elmstone Hardwicke to Guiting, and scotched its wheels on the village green. With great magnanimity the vicar and the monks, whose monastery door opens to the green, accorded the missioners a welcome to the village, but a curious scene followed the meeting in the evening. This missioner held an open-air meeting, which was attended by nearly all the villagers, young and old, but when it was over, one of the monks (said to be Father Drake, and erstwhile curate of the parish) mounted the monastery wall and attempted to address the meeting. He was immediately greeted with a loud outburst of jeers from the excited crowd, and after an argument lasting an hour missiles were thrown (some of which were broken on the door emitting an odour which to say the least was not savoury), and the parties nearly came to blows. Sufficient to mention that the quarrel lasted so long that it was well past midnight when the villagers returned to their homes.

No one had been hurt though the wordy warfare had been so loud and long.

*Cheltenham Free Press*
2 July 1898

# All Satisfied

In any conversation with the oldsters of Tytherington there will inevitably be much talk of Squire Hardwicke, and of that other great man, George Boyt, pork butcher and founder of the Baptist chapel. Arthur Boyt, his descendant, was just getting ready to go to chapel when I called on him, but he met me with a cheery smile and invited me in. His grandfather was one of those excellent old preachers who were not only good Christians but fine orators, and, occasionally, wits. Arthur told me that his grandfather was highly respected locally, and could be a formidable opponent. If he had a notion he hadn't seen some villager in chapel, he would make a point of stopping him next day and ask him what he thought of the sermon. His sermons were remarkable for their homely analogies. For instance he used to say that some men, like pigs, never bothered to look up until they were on their backs.

George Boyt did not love parsons. In his day they were all too often university men who regarded the church as a profession, and used their pulpit for expounding the rightness of the existing order. Like many free-churchmen he had cause to resent the power and prestige of the rector who had been foisted on them by the squire; but, unlike most of his contemporaries, he could turn the situation into a joke. He would tell the story of a stranger coming into a certain village (he would say where), to find a funeral in progress. Enquiring of bystanders whose funeral it was, the man is told it's old parson's. Curious about the cause of death, he asks: 'Any complaints?' ... 'No, no sir,' echo the guileless locals. 'We'em all satisfied!'

Lewis Wilshire
*The Vale of Berkeley* (1954)

# An Awful Occurrence

An awful occurrence took place at Blakeney the 24th January 1796. The Rev. William Bishop of Gloucester went to deliver a weekly lecture; he had no sooner commenced the service than an attempt was made to interrupt him by the mistress of the next house, who procured a fiddle and held a country dance, the noise of which was kept up upon the same floor, and within four or five feet of the preacher, so near are the houses. On the next day a very striking event happened – This woman was taken ill in the morning, and a corpse at night.

Revd John Horlick
*A Visit to the Forest of Dean*, 1835

# A Hoax

The best news that I have ever learnt here is, that the Botley parson is become quite a gentle creature, compared to what he used to be. The people in the village have told me some most ridiculous stories about his having been hoaxed in London! It seems that somebody danced him up from Botley to London, by telling him that a legacy had been left him, or some such story. Up went the parson on horseback, being in too great a hurry to run the risk of coach. The hoaxers, it appears, got him to some hotel, and there set upon him a whole tribe of applicants: wet-nurses, dry-nurses, lawyers with deeds of conveyance for borrowed money, curates in want of churches, coffin-makers, travelling companions, ladies' maids, dealers in Yorkshire hams, Newcastle coals, and dealers in dried night-soil at Islington. In short, I am rightly informed, they kept the parson in town for several days, bothered him three parts out of his senses, compelled him to escape, as it were, from a fire; and then, when he got home, he found the village posted all over with handbills giving an account of his adventure, under the pretence of offering 500 pounds reward, for a discovery of the hoaxers!

William Cobbett, 5 August 1823
*Rural Rides*

# 'Water, Sir!'

Then the Vicar of Fordington told us of the state of things in his parish when he first came to it nearly half a century ago. No man had ever been known to receive the Holy Communion except the parson, the clerk and the sexton. There were 16 women communicants and most of them went away when he refused to pay them for coming. They had been accustomed there at some place in the neighbourhood to pass the cup to each other with a nod of the head. At one church there were two male communicants. When the cup was given to the first he touched his forelock and said, 'Here's the good health of our Lord Jesus Christ.'

One day there was christening and no water in the Font. 'Water, Sir!' said the clerk in astonishment. 'The last parson never used no water. He spit into his hand.' Prostitutes and persons keeping houses of ill fame offered themselves as sponsors and were astonished and aggrieved when they were refused. The Holy Communion was administered only three times a year. An old woman being asked how many Sacraments there were in the Church of England replied, 'Three; there is the Christmas Sacrament, the Easter Sacrament and the Whitsuntide Sacrament.'

Francis Kilvert, Thursday, May Eve, 1874
*Diaries*

# Sunday Wreck

In former times, when a ship was being driven on the rocks on Sunday, whilst divine service was going on, news was sent to the parson, who announced the fact from the pulpit, or reading desk, whereupon ensued a rapid clearance of the church. The story is told of a parson at Ponghill, near Morwenstow, who, on hearing the news, proceeded down the nave in his surplice as far as the font; and the people, supposing there was to be a christening, did not stir. But when he was near the door he shouted: 'My Christian brethren, there's a ship wrecked in the

cove; let us all start fair!' and, flinging off his surplice, led the
way to the scene of spoliation.

S. Baring Gould
*The Vicar of Morwenstow*

# Who Is A-Gwain to Prache?

A retired country parson wrote the other day and told me a story
about a parish in his neighbourhood where a young curate was
appointed to assist a vicar full of years. The latter went off to a
service one day to find the congregation in the churchyard. He
asked one of the men what it all meant. 'Well, zur, we be come
to zee whether thee bist a-gwain to prache or whether the young
man be a-gwain to prache. If the young man be a-gwain to
prache, we be a-gwain to stop: if thee bist a-gwain to prache, we
be a-gwain whoam.'

H.J. Massingham
*A Countryman's Journal* (1939)

# Local Preacher

I remember one old local preacher, named Maslin, who used to
come to the chapel now and then, clad in a white smock
reaching halfway below the knees. This old fellow was an
agricultural labourer, and lived far away over the downs. He was
very short in stature, with grey hair and exceedingly bronzed and
sunburnt; he had toiled among the sheep and lambs, the wheat
and oats, and had heard the lark sing in the blue heavens
thousands of times. He had also felt the cold nipping wind
sweeping up the valley and over the hilltops, and had trudged
through the deep snow to the village over and over again. When
he came to preach he carried his dinner tied up in a red
handkerchief and hung on a blackthorn stick over his shoulder.
His fare was very simple – bread and cheese, and he must have a
glass of ale with it from somewhere or other; he did not indulge

in hot cooked food that day. A great number used to go and hear him preach; he could always command a congregation, he was so sternly simple, outspoken and comical. He was a firm believer in the devil as a personality. Once when he had been called to see a sick man, and had not been able to make a very deep impression on the unfortunate, he attributed it all to the actual presence of the Evil One. 'I know'd 'a was ther,' the old man declared most gravely, 'for I could smell the brimstone; the house was full on't.'

One Sunday evening, in late autumn, he was down to preach, and there was the usual full attendance; the little chapel was packed; a great time was expected; they were not all disappointed. Old Maslin was beside himself, and preached vehemently. As the sermon proceeded – it was half sermon and half prayer – he waxed hotter and hotter. Now he leaned far forward over the pulpit, now jumped backward, stamped hard with his feet, and swayed from side to side. The congregation perspired, and trembled in their pews. Louder and louder the old fellow's voice pealed out; he stamped harder and harder; everyone felt something was to happen, and happen it did. There was a large iron stove in that chapel; it stood in the centre. The pipes from this went up and then passed horizontally to the wall some distance away. Moreover, they had not been swept out for a long time, and were become very foul. The storm raged with increasing fury. The old folk were getting uncomfortable; the young girls tittered. The preacher shouted at the top of his voice, and stamped mightily with his feet. 'Send the power, and send it now!' he cried. One more moment, and it came. The joints of the pipes could stand no longer. With a shuddering crack the whole lot of the horizontals toppled down. A loud yell went up from the people; the youth exploded; but there were no heads broken. There was a prompt young man sitting just underneath that pipe. At the first crack he leapt up and caught it falling; but he made a sinister use of the opportunity. Receiving the pipes in the middle, with a dexterous movement of the hands, he twirled them round, and shot vast clouds of soot over all the people from one end of the place to the other. The result may be better imagined than described; it was like a pandemonium.

Alfred Williams
*A Wiltshire Village* (1912)

# A Sign

My earliest recollection of my father was that he was a rather quiet kindly man of few words, with a great sense of integrity, to whom the very thought of an underhand action was abhorrent. As a country priest he was confidant, friend and consoler of all who came to him in trouble, and as a sportsman he was the delight of the farmers with whom he shot, in the field or on the range. Despite his great ability with gun or rifle he was the soul of modesty, making light of his many successes in both shooting competitions or on a partridge drive. Our long walks together in the country were always full of pleasure and interest. He knew every bird and animal, their nesting and breeding habits, where to find them at any time of the day or night. Few people had greater love of the countryside or were better informed about all its denizens, and he had a wealth of anecdotes to tell about his own experiences.

One of his most dedicated tasks was visiting the sick, and two of his stories about such visits have always remained with me. On one occasion he visited a recently bereaved widow who invited him into the house and said, 'I had a strange experience last night, Sir. I was sitting by the fire when my late husband came in, sat in his usual chair, picked up the Bible and read a verse or two, after which he fared to vanish. What do you think was the reason for that?'

My father replied, 'I expect you had been thinking a great deal about your late husband and conjured up a vision of him.'

'That's not what my neighbour do say,' replied the widow.

'Oh, what did your neighbour say?' my father enquired.

'She do say it be a sign of rain, Sir.'

J.A.N. Fitt
*The Bob Man* (Moonraker Press, 1977)

## No Thank You

'Who's that at this hour in the morning,' said Mother, scrambling up and heading for the door.

'No thank you,' we heard her say. She was more definite than usual. 'I never buy tracts. I'm not interested in them. I have my Bible.'

'Most people have Bibles, but they don't read them,' said the man.

'I do not happen to be one of them,' said Mother crisply.

'Reading the Good Book is not enough,' he went on, and I thought what a fool he was to argue with Mother.

'It isn't easy to understand its teaching. The layman is not fitted to comprehend its great message. That is why I am here. To explain to you some of the Great Mysteries. That is what my papers are about; to point out the only true way to Salvation!'

'Just a minute,' said Mother. There was an edge on her voice, and she spoke slowly. I knew her eyes were growing dark.

'Don't misunderstand me, Madam,' said the man quickly. 'I have come to give you good news. The news that you may be saved. You, your husband and all your little children ... those dear, innocent little kiddies, conceived in sin ...'

'How dare you!' cried Mother. 'How dare you make insinuations like that! Let me tell you that I was brought up on the teaching of the Bible. And I know a great deal more about it than you ever will. My children have been brought up on it too. I just will not tolerate total strangers coming to my house and telling me what I should believe at nine o'clock in the morning!'

'I am obliged to warn you that you will be damned! You'll be damned. All of you ... doomed to be thrown into the pit of fire and brimstone ... doomed to the everlasting torments of hell ...'

Mother sniffed. 'We are all entitled to our opinions,' she said. 'And now you'd better go before I lose my temper.'

Marooned on our chairs we looked at one another and said nothing.

'And one more thing,' said Mother. 'Don't you go calling next door. Everybody's out. Except an old lady over eighty. And she won't be interested. Don't you dare go frightening her with your blood and thunder.'

She slammed the door and the house shuddered. We heard her snorting on the doormat. There was a scuffle of steps and she went swiftly up the hall, unbolted the door and rushed out. We knew where she'd gone and heard her thudding through Granny's kitchen, towards the back door.

She reached it in time to answer the knock.

'I thought I told you not to come here?' she cried and I would have given anything to have seen the man's face at this confrontation.

'Call yourself a religious man! Going about frightening poor old ladies to death! Clear off, double quick, before I call the police ...'

There was the sound of his footsteps on the pitchen, the slam of a door and then mother's steps, thudding through the cottage again.

When she returned she was red in the face. Deep strands of her hair fell from the clip.

'The very idea!' she exploded as she got on with the scrubbing. 'Whatever will people get up to next! I've no objection to them selling tracts if they really believe in what they're doing. But that man! Only last week he was working for a bookmaker in North Street. He got the sack for sticking to the takings. Who's he, for goodness sake, to go round telling ordinary God-fearing people they'll end up in fire and brimstone. He'll know all about that if he goes on the way he's going!'

Mavis Budd
*Fit For A Duchess* (1970)

# 6 December 1791

This being my Tithe Audit Day, the following People waited on me, paid me their respective dues and dined and spent the remaining part of the day with me, they left me about 12 o'clock at night, well pleased with their entertainment. Mr Girling and son, Mr Peachman, Mr Howlett, John Baker, Jonas Silvey, Henry Case, Js. Pegg, Robt. Emeris, Stephen Andrews, Hugh Bush, Willm. Bidewell, John Buck, John Norton, Thos. Reynolds Junr., John Culley, Charles Hardy, Henry Rising, Thos. Carey, and John Heavers. Widow Pratts Son James came soon after dinner and paid me for his Mother.

He came quite drunk and behaved very impudently. Stephen Andrews and Billy Bidewell rather full. Billy Bidewell paid me for a Calf which he is to have of me in a few days 0.10.6. Reed.

for tithe today about 285.0.0. I gave them for Dinner a Surloin of Beef rosted, Sliff-Marrow-Bone of Beef boiled, a boiled Leg of Mutton and Caper Sauce, a couple of Rabbits and Onion Sauce, Some Salt Fish boiled and Parsnips and Egg Sauce with plenty of Plumb-Puddings and plain ditto. They spoke highly in favour of my strong Beer, they never drank any better they said. Paid Stephen Andrews for Carr[iage] of Coal 0.15.0. Paid Ditto, for 1½d Rate to the Church 0.2.0. Recd. of Ditto, my last Visitation Fee. 0.2.6. Mr Howlett was very dull and dejected. There was drank, six Bottles of Rum which made three Bowls of Punch, four Bottles of Port Wine, besides strong-Beer. No Punch or Wine suffered in Kitchen.

James Woodforde
*The Diary of a Country Parson*

# Turnips

A farmer sent word to the Vicar that on a certain day he would be turnip hauling. The day arrived – so did the parson's cart to collect his tenth. Both carts went to the turnip field together. The farmer then threw nine turnips into his own cart and one into the parson's cart, with the words: 'That's all the turnip hauling I'm doing to-day, my man. Good morning!' One man, one horse, one cart and one turnip returned to the Vicarage. An expensive turnip!

*Facts and Figures of an Unequal Struggle*
(Ashford, Kent and Sussex Tithepayers' Association, *c.* 1948)

# Bees

One day a parson visiting a farmer remarked: 'Oh, I see you have ten stocks of bees. As you know, my friend, one stock belongs to me.'

'No, no!' said the farmer, 'bees are different. I shall not surrender one tenth of these.'

But the parson persisted, and after a while the farmer gave in, saying: 'All right! I'll bring one along this evening.'

'Thank you, my good man,' says the parson, and departed.

At dusk the farmer took a sheet and shook a swarm of bees into it, went to the parsonage, knocked at the door and asked for the Vicar. When he appeared at the door, the farmer dropped two corners, holding the other two, and with a shake of the sheet towards the Vicar, cries out: 'Here's your tithe delivered. Good night!'

*Facts and Figures of an Unequal Struggle*
(Ashford, Kent and Sussex Tithepayers' Association, *c.* 1948)

# Babies

A member of the Committee of the Ashford, Kent and Sussex Tithepayers' Association, tells that his father was taken to the parson as the tenth baby, the mother saying: 'This is yours, as I understand that you claim one-tenth of everything.' The parson gave the mother two five pound notes to take the crying babe back home. This child had the best education of the village, receiving lessons to fourteen years of age. His mother had only three days' schooling and she died at the age of eighty-six.

*Facts and Figures of an Unequal Struggle*
(Ashford, Kent and Sussex Tithepayers' Association, *c.* 1948)

# Two Hens and One Egg

In 1932 a determined raid was made on a number of farms near Canterbury to collect stock for unpaid tithes. It was reported that police assembled in quiet country lanes – many of them dressed as labourers – to be ready for the first sign of trouble. Needless to say the farmers had made preparations too.

While fifty police were bring brought 'secretly' into this district in two large furniture vans, they became involved in a collision. One of the vans ran away down a steep hill and collided with the other, finishing up in a ditch near the police station. Five men remained suffering from bruises and slight shock.

When the farmers and villagers ran to the scene they were amazed to find that the vans were filled with police.

The first call was at Stonebridge Farm. A solicitor accompanied by a bailiff and two police sergeants, called at the farm with a large lorry to take away three impounded cows but these animals could not be found and the lorry went empty away.

Similar incidents happened at other farms.

As the lorry went from farm to farm the van-loads of police moved from one strategic point to another and disguised motor police patrolled the roads, to assist these modern tithe-collectors.

At River Farm however, the party met with a certain amount of success. Here, distress had been levied on twenty-five White Leghorns, and the onlookers were highly amused in watching the bailiff trying to catch the fowls as they flew squawking in every direction. The boys and girls screamed as the Court bailiff fell flat in the mud in trying to seize one elusive bird.

Eventually, two hens were captured, but the owner made a formal protest to the police as one was the wrong breed; the birds were however placed in the lorry, but the excitement proved too much for one hen and it laid an egg.

After six hours, no further success was recorded, so the lorry departed for London with two hens and one egg.

*Facts and Figures of an Unequal Struggle*
(Ashford, Kent and Sussex Tithepayers' Association, *c.* 1948)

# Trouble at the Farm

Trouble at this farm has been brewing for some months. Tithe to the value of £127 for the year 1930 is owing, and the authorities had impounded eight stacks, which, meanwhile, had been sold by tender. These stacks are stated to have been valued by a well-known firm of Stowmarket auctioneers at £340, and at meetings of the Suffolk Tithepayers' Association members were exhorted to make a mass demonstration when the stacks were seized. A surprise was attempted on the part of the authorities. They notified the police and contractors only, and when these turned up at 6.30 in the morning they had the place to themselves. However, telephone messages soon apprised sympathisers, and by mid-day there was a crowd of three hundred congesting the narrow lane which belongs to the Hall Farm. The bells of the parish church were rung by three women, to give notification to the village. One woman was Mrs Western, herself the widow of a clergyman before her present marriage. The rector of Elmsett, the Rev. C.F.B. Haslewood, was away for the day. There were fifty cars on the high road. They came every few minutes, bringing farmers from all parts of the county, and from Essex and Norfolk. Farmers in the neighbourhood of Elmsett gave their men the day off to swell the demonstration.

Things began to quicken by the middle of the morning. Hitherto the haulage men had been hampered only by insistent requests to stop their lorries to allow farm vehicles to come through. On the face of it the demands were reasonable, if a bit frequent and awkward. A trench had been dug in front of the gate that led into the farmyard, and it was not possible for a lorry to enter until it was filled. But there again the ostensible reason for digging the trench was to inspect a pipe which carried the ditch water underneath. Now a farm tractor was requisitioned to drag a large fowl-house from its moorings and to plant it just where the private lane enters the highway. The wheels were taken off and there it sat, squat and large and stubbornly obstructive. A small elm tree was sawn through. It was ready to crash across the lane, except that the branches were strongly entangled in those of a much larger elm. So farm hands set to work to fell the big elm, using a large amount of zeal, but a somewhat inadequate two-handled saw. They were probably relieved when half-an-hour later they were notified that the contractors had decided to withdraw their lorries.

One of the lorries was then borrowed as a platform for Mr Western, Mr P.J.Butler (secretary of the Suffolk Tithepayers' Association) and Mr Makens Turner. Speeches were partly congratulatory and partly regretful. They thanked people for support, and expressed willingness to pay tithe so long as it was on a basis which was not 'economically impossible'. Mr Western explained his position. He stated that his accounts, audited by a firm of chartered accountants showed a loss of £350 for last year. He had offered £50 out of his capital to satisfy tithe, but this had been refused, and they had impounded £340 worth of stuff for £127 debt.

*Suffolk Chronicle and Mercury*
6 May 1932

# Which Waspe

When the tithe war was on, the Commissioners tried to extract the tithe which was owing on a certain farm. Tithe is paid by the landlord and they couldn't find out who the landlord was. The land was farmed by two old brothers called Waspe. They said they didn't own the farm, only farmed it. The commissioners brought an action to recover the tithe. The two Waspe brothers were witnesses. The Church briefed a clever barrister from London. When one of the brothers was in the witness-box, he was closely cross-examined. First he was asked his name. It took him a little time to recollect this. Then he was asked what his mother's name was. That was a puzzle – 'Well, we always call her Mum,' he said. The examination went on for about two hours during which time counsel elicited no information whatever. Finally, counsel asked: 'Are there any other Waspes in your village?' A beatific smile spread over the man's face – 'Hundreds and thousands on 'em,' he said.

Some time later the Commissioner did find out the truth – the old mother was the owner and they got judgement against her. They were entitled at law to seize the produce of the farm but they were not entitled to harvest the crops. So the two old brothers left the corn unharvested and the birds had the harvest.

Justin and Edith Brooke
*Suffolk Prospect* (1963)

# Friends

Mr Ernest John Thorne of Church Farm, Coombe Bissett, near Salisbury, walked out of Winchester gaol on Thursday, a free man once again. Sent there the previous day for contempt of court, for not complying with a county court order to pay tithe arrears, he was released after his fellow farmers collected the £37.7s.6d arrears and paid it to the prison governor. The 'rescue party' of 30 farmers and their wives came from Dorset, Wiltshire and Hampshire, and gave Mr Thorne three cheers as he joined them. Mr. E.V.E. Parson, chairman of the Salisbury branch, National Tithe Association, who was in the party, told a Press Reporter: 'Mr Thorne is the first martyr to fight this iniquity. We shall carry on the fight until victory.' Mr Thorne said he was treated with every courtesy in prison. When he was not in his cell he lectured the warders on tithes.

*Wiltshire Gazette*
16 August 1945

# Dues, 1821

Being engaged to meet Feare before the Magistrates to prove my title to the tithes of the colliers' gardens, which were originally taken from the farm, I went to Bath soon after breakfast. Sir Robert Baker and Mr Clarke, the Mayor, were the only magistrates present. On producing my Tithe Book the magistrates told Feare he had no plea whatever in withholding from Clarke the dues which I have given him, and asked him his motives for so doing. The man replied he wished to see Mr Skinner's agreement with the Coal Company, and that was the reason he desired the men to withhold their payments. I said his reason was to set the colliers against me and render unpopular a measure which I intended for their good, as Clarke, the Schoolmaster, had his tithe for keeping a Sunday School to which all the colliers might send their children. On leaving the hall, I told Feare I was convinced he meant to set the colliers against me: that it was most impolite his so doing, since I had always been very careful to advise this body of men to be obedient to the agents employed to superintend them, and that I well knew the evil of stirring up sedition among so numerous a class of men, and that even when they made their just complaints against some of the late bailiffs who had defrauded them I still recommended their obedience for the general benefit of society. He said he was sure he had never meant to set the people against me, and should not in future induce them to withhold their dues.

John Skinner
*Journal of a Somerset Rector 1803-1834* (1984)

# The Gentry

# Telling the Tenantry

The preparations for the approaching election furnish us with indisputable proof of the necessity for some better protection for voters than the present machinery, despite the innovations of last session, is capable of affording. The Manchester Examiner tells the following tale of intimidation, in reference to the voters on the estate of Mr Warburton, of Arley in Mid-Cheshire. The information is contained in a letter from Mr Lewis Ashworth of Manchester and this is the story Mr Ashworth has to tell:

'Mr Warburton, of Arley, has seventy or eighty tenants on his estate, each of whom has a vote. His steward, Donald, has been to each voter, and has told each that the landlord will inform the tenantry of how they are to vote, and that their votes must be given as he may dictate. Moreover Mr Warburton has personally waited upon Mr Fair, a leading farmer in the district, and after censuring him for taking the liberty of canvassing the Arley tenants, told him (Fair) that he would tell the tenants which way they were to vote, and that Mr Warren should not have one vote from that estate. On Monday night I saw one tenant, who is a very intelligent man, and he assured me he should be glad to assist Warren, but if he as much as gave liberty for the address of Warren to be stuck up on the property, he would have 'notice to quit' to-morrow. He said that the tenantry would be taken to vote like a flock of sheep and that not one of them dare think for himself.

*Gloucester Journal*
12 September 1868

# Walks with Thomas Hardy

I went to Max Gate with a good luncheon basket, and collected him and Florence Hardy. My wife and son sat with her at the back, and T.H. was beside me at the wheel. 'Now, T.H.,' I said, 'where do you want to go?' He thought for a while. Then he said he would like to go to High Stoy, that hill in west Dorset made famous in 'The Woodlanders'. While I was driving down one of the country lanes, T.H. said, 'Go slow here. I want you to notice this woman coming towards us.' When she had passed he said, 'That might have been Tess. That is just how I imagined her to be.'

At the bottom of the hill we ate our lunch. Then T.H. said he wanted to climb the hill. I was nervous about this. He had passed the age of eighty. Was I going to be responsible for the death of the greatest figure in literature at that time? But he would do it, and did. When he came down, fresh as a lark, he told me he would never climb High Stoy again. And he was right.

On the way home, as we drove near Cerne Abbas, he asked me to stop the car. 'See that farm over there, and that big field?' he said. 'Kipling came down to stay with me a short time ago, and wanted to go over the scenes of my novels. So I brought him round here. When we were crossing that big field there on foot, a savage sow came for us. We made a dash for the hedge, and were scrambling through it when the farmer came out and shouted, 'Let 'un be! Let 'un be! 'E won't 'urt 'ee, if 'ee don't rumple 'un.' Said Hardy, 'We weren't waiting to rumple 'un.' And he added, 'Kipling and I tore our suits to pieces getting through that hedge.'

Sir Newman Flower
*The Countryman*, winter 1945

# Days with A.J. Munnings

[An incident from the 1930s.] Immediately Munnings revived, and started one of his ballads. So we rollicked along in the old yellow car, with occasional imprecatory gestures at some herds of Friesian cows, those 'damned unpaintable cattle', till we came to Halesworth. There he bought a pint of shrimps. Thence we continued along the Roman road to Bungay, shrimp heads flying, ballad still going strong.

That may have been the day when we went to view Kirstead Old Hall, which Munnings had a fancy he might buy, to get back into his native Norfolk. On that occasion I was cast for the role of intending purchaser, Maurice Codner, the portrait painter, who was out with us, was co-opted to impersonate an architect, Munnings himself to pose as a mere friend, because he said that if his name were revealed the price would probably be stepped up sharply.

My impersonation of a man of means lacked conviction, and Codner rather overplayed his part, I thought; jabbing his pen-knife into sound beams and muttering about settlements.

One day, as we journeyed, Munnings told me he had adopted a Hay diet. At that time I had not heard of Dr Hay. I just gaped, knowing how much of his life was horses anyway. As I munched my sandwiches of bread and beef, he said, 'That's the worst thing for you if you only knew it: the stomach can't cope with starch and protein at the same time.'

But I went on munching unalarmed, while he fought his way through a huge cos lettuce. 'You'll kill yourself eating that stuff,' he added – rather enviously, I thought.

I stayed with him on Exmoor too, and we roamed the Coleridge country. At Nether Stowey we found some excellent local cider at twopence a glass. It tasted innocuous. But suddenly Munnings banged his fist down on the table. The cider was not so mild, I realized. On leaving he cried to the assembled company in the inn, 'You ought to be as happy as lords here; you can get drunk for fourpence.'

Adrian Bell
*My Own Master* (1961)

# A Ploughman's Day with A.J.M.

Billy Munnings was born at Mendham Mill, the eldest of four brothers, one of whom was the artist, and here was an example of the brotherly love to be expected in a farming family on the Norfolk-Suffolk border. William Green Munnings, to give him his full name, was himself an artist in the breeding of outstanding dairy cows and Suffolk horses, and won many prizes, but his famous brother was always 'that bugger' to him. They were both forthright. One letter from Sir Alfred that W.G. showed me started off, without any preamble, – 'How long are you going to keep on barking and yapping ...' and went on like that for several pages. Many the stories that W.G. told me about A.J. One about the artist stopping a ploughman at work in a field on W.G.'s farm, and sitting there painting him and his horses all day. 'What'll my master say?' protested the ploughman. 'Hell with him,' said A.J., 'but here's a bob for yourself.'

B.A. Steward
*One Journey* (1981)

# A Visit

A young film director did once write to me that his company was considering basing a film on my rural trilogy, and could he come down and talk it over with me?

Marjorie and I thought; this is wonderful news. I was trying to farm a clay farm I had bought cheap because a third of it had gone out of cultivation and I was very short of cash.

So the film director came for the week-end, and Marjorie put flowers in the spare room. When he had unpacked his bag, had a drink and a good supper, and was warming his toes at our fire, he announced that he had not really any idea of making a film out of my book: he had simply wanted to spend a day or two in the country.

I wondered whether to throw him out, but Marjorie gave me a steadying look, and I just laughed it off. I had thought of a better plan, prompted by a throw-away remark of his about needing fresh air and exercise. We were at the time cutting down a thorn hedge of over twenty years' growth. Next day I set him to work on it beside me. I kept on all day till dark, ending with an enormous bonfire of thorns and brambles.

I was glad to see him clutch his lumbar region as he hoisted himself into his train the next day. He held out a hand scored with scratches, and smiled from under singed eyebrows as he said good-bye. That was my one and only contact with a film director.

Adrian Bell
*My Own Master* (1961)

# The Eccentric John Mytton

John Mytton (1796-1834). Squire of Halston, Shropshire, ex-MP for Shrewsbury, High Sheriff for the counties of Shropshire and Merioneth, Major of the North Shropshire Yeomanry Cavalry. He inherited a large fortune and squandered it and was imprisoned for debt. His eccentric and daring exploits were legion.

In the saddle too, he ran prodigious risks for his life, not only by riding at apparently impracticable fences, with hounds, but in falling from his horse when intoxicated. For the former of these acts he was for many years so notorious, that it was a common answer to the question – whether a certain sort of fence could be leaped, or whether any man would attempt it? – that it would do for Mytton. He once actually galloped at full speed over a rabbit warren, to try whether or not his horse would fall, which of course he did, and rolled over him. This perfect contempt of danger was truly characteristic of himself; but, not content with the possession of it, he endeavoured to impart it to his friends. As he was one day driving one of them in a gig, who expressed a strong regard for his neck, with a hint that he considered it in some danger, Mytton addressed him thus: – 'Was you ever much hurt then, by being upset in a gig?' 'No, thank God,' said his companion, 'for I never was upset in one.' 'What!' replied Mytton – 'never upset in a gig? What a d—d slow fellow you must have been all your life;' and, running his near wheel up the bank, over they both went, fortunately without either being much injured!

But Mr Mytton appeared, at least wished to be supposed to be, indifferent to pain. A very few days after he had had so bad a fall with his own hounds as to occasion the dislocation of three ribs, and was otherwise much bruised, a friend in Wales, unconscious of his accident, sent him a fox in a bag, with a hint that, if turned out on the morrow, he would be sure to afford sport, as he was only just caught. 'Tomorrow, then,' said Mytton, 'will we run him'; and although he was lifted upon his horse, having his body swathed with rollers, and also writhing with pain, he took the lead of all the field upon a horse he called 'The Devil,' and was never headed by any man, till he killed the fox, at the end of a capital hour's run. He was very near fainting from the severity of this trial; but I remember him telling me, he would not have been seen to faint for ten thousand pounds.

Returning from hunting one day, he, with some others, called to lunch at a farm-house called the Berries, near Whitchurch, where there was a very large and savage dog chained in the yard. 'Pray don't go near him, Mr Mytton,' said the owner, 'for he will tear you in pieces if you do.' This was enough for Mytton; so pulling a silk handkerchief out of the pocket of a friend, and lapping it around his left hand, he advanced with it extended towards the dog, who immediately seized it with his mouth ... Catching him by the back of the neck however, with his right hand, Mytton immediately pinned the animal by the nose with his teeth; and getting the other hand at liberty, so pummelled his opponent that he had scarcely any life left in him.

... did you ever hear of a man setting fire to his own shirt, to frighten away the hiccup? Such, however, is the climax I have alluded to; and this is the manner in which it was performed: 'D—n this hiccup,' said Mytton, as he stood undressed on the floor, apparently in the act of getting into his bed; 'but I'll frighten it away;' so seizing a lighted candle, applied it to the tail of his shirt, and – it being a cotton one – he was instantly enveloped in flames.

Now, how was his life saved? is the next question that might be asked. Why, by the active exertions of his London customer, and of another stout and intrepid young man that happened to be in the room, who jointly threw him down on the ground and tore his shirt from his body, piecemeal. Then, here again comes John Mytton! 'The hiccup is gone by —,' said he, and reeled, naked, into his bed.

Some of Mytton's practical jokes were rather 'beyond a joke' – or in other words, he would sometimes 'drive the jest too far.' For example. He had the wire of a spring gun laid in the path, in his shrubbery at Halston, which he knew his chaplain would take on his road to church. So soon as he heard the report, for which he was of course on the watch, he ran out of the house and accused the parson of shooting at his pheasants on a Sunday. His reverence's nerves, however, were so disturbed by the shock, that he was unable to face his congregation until he returned to the house and composed himself. Mytton's universal remedy was proposed by him, and two glasses of Madeira made the parson all right again.

Nimrod

*The Life of John Mytton* (Rudolph Ackerman, 1837; Methuen, 9th edition, 1949)

# Beans

It was in a field nearby that Sir Maurice Berkeley was once discomfited. The story was told me by Mr P.G. Davies, who in his turn was told it by his wife. Mrs Davies' father farmed Wanswell Court Farm up to about seventy-two years ago, and her mother was the daughter of John Cary of Ham Green Farm, Berkeley, and the licensee of the Berkeley Arms Hotel. Her sister married John Ayris, who was huntsman to the Berkeley Hunt. Anyway, the story goes that Sir Maurice was cub-hunting one day, and had drawn several coverts without success, when the hunt came to a field of beans near Wanswell.

'You'd better draw those beans,' Sir Maurice instructed the huntsman.

'I shouldn't put the hounds in there, Sir. They beans is dead ripe,' said the huntsman, and he was backed up by the farmer who was standing nearby.

'Oh, they won't do any harm,' Sir Maurice said airily, more interested in sport than good husbandry.

Into the field went the hounds, killed seven cubs, and made a frightful mess of the crop. Seeing that the damage was considerable, Sir Maurice rode up to the farmer, who was still standing by, and said: 'Afraid the hounds have made rather a mess of your beans.'

'Yes, they have knocked 'em about a bit. But they bain't my beans, Sir Maurice.'

'No? Whose are they then?'

'Yours, sir. I sold them to your steward this morning.'

Lewis Wilshire<br>*The Vale of Berkeley* (1954)

108

# The Ladies

One of the chief inhibitions of the rural community into which we came as a family in 1921, was the convention that 'ladies' should seem to be unaware of the facts of life. 'Ladies' in this context included every woman above the status of peasant, though even the labourer's wife would have had her susceptibilities spared by the master and mistress if it were possible.

For instance, elaborate precautions were taken at Farley Hall when the stud stallion was due on the farm, that the 'missis' did not inadvertently come upon the scene. (So gross a matter could not even be mentioned to her as impending, to warn her to keep out of the way.) And once that awful conjunction occurred. I shall never forget the consternation. There was the Suffolk stallion mounted on the mare, magnificent as a figure in a Parthenon frieze. Round the corner of the yard appeared at that moment not only Mrs Colville, but also two refined female friends whom she had brought out to show her turkeys.

Afterwards I found Mr Colville pacing up and down in a sweat muttering, 'A nice thing for ladies to see, I must say!'

Adrian Bell
*My Own Master* (1961)

# The Wisdom of the Duke

Now and again he [the Duke] could exhibit the Wisdom of Solomon. Some years ago an eccentric Master of Foxhounds died, leaving in his Will a clause stating that on his death he wished to be fed to his hounds.

The distraught lawyer sought advice from Master [the Duke] on his embarrassing predicament.

Master solved the problem without delay. Quick as a flash came the solution. 'Cremate him,' the lawyer was told, 'and then sprinkle his ashes over the broth in the troughs.' And, to the best of my knowledge, it was so ...

Daphne Moore
'Reminiscences of the Tenth Duke of Beaufort'
*Gloucestershire – The County Magazine*, October 1986

# John Ruskin Obtains Silence

From the aesthetic standpoint uncouth and noisy machines, such as mowers and reapers, cannot be compared to a lusty team of men with scythes, in their white shirts, backed by the flowering meadows; or a sunny field of busy harvesters facing a golden wall of corn, and leaving behind them the fresh-shorn stubble dotted with sheaves and nicely balanced shocks. The rattle of the machines, too, is discordant and out of harmony with the peaceful countryside.

It is related of Ruskin that, hearing the insistent rattle of a mowing machine in a meadow adjoining his home by the beautiful Coniston Water, and his sense of the fitting being outraged, he interviewed the owner, and, by an offer to pay the trifling difference between machine and hand labour, induced him to discontinue the annoyance.

A.H. Savory (Blackwell, 1920)
*Grain and Chaff from an English Manor*

# Not in Front of the Castle

An amusing story is told of Castle Meadow, the last of the flat, wide water-meadows immediately adjacement to the Castle. Part of it lies under the Castle walls, and is therefore within observation from the windows, so that a former Steward of the Berkeleys was surprised to come across Old Jim pitching hay minus his trousers.

'Jim! Jim!' he apostrophised. 'You can't work in front of the Castle without any trousers on. Not in front of the Castle, Jim! Whatever made you leave 'em off?'

'Well, zur,' said Jim, 'we tapped a vresh cask o' zider this marnin. An' you do know what vresh zider be, main zurchin. It've bin servin' I out crool, an' I've took me trousis down so often I thought 'twood save time, like, if I lef' em off altogether … just until the zider have a' done workin' me.'

Normally, any scheme for saving time would have recommended itself to the Steward, but there were exceptions, and this was one of them. 'Not in front of the Castle, Jim,' he said, reprovingly. 'You must remember where you are.'

Lewis Wilshire
*The Vale of Berkeley* (1954)

# Country Crime

# Old Wiltshire Days

It is surprising to find how very few the real crimes were in those days, despite the misery of the people; that nearly all the 'crimes' for which men were sentenced to the gallows and to transportation for life, or for long terms, were offences which would now be sufficiently punished by a few weeks', or even a few days', imprisonment. Thus in April 1825 I note that Mr Justice Park commented on the heavy appearance of the calendar. It was not so much the number (170) of the offenders that excited his concern as it was the nature of the crimes with which they were charged. The worst crime in this instance was sheep-stealing!

Again, this same Mr Justice Park, at the Spring Assizes at Salisbury, 1827, said that though the calendar was a heavy one, he was happy to find on looking at the deposition of the principal cases, that they were not of a very serious character. Nevertheless he passed sentence of death on twenty-eight persons, among them being one for stealing half a crown!

Of the twenty-eight all but three were eventually reprieved, one of the fated three being a youth of nineteen, who was charged with stealing a mare and pleaded guilty in spite of a warning from the judge not to do so. This irritated the great man who had the power of life and death in his hand. In passing sentence the judge 'expatiated on the prevalence of the crime of horse-stealing and the necessity of making an example. The enormity of Read's crime rendered him a proper example, and he would therefore hold out no hope of mercy towards him.' As to the plea of guilty, he remarked that nowadays too many persons pleaded guilty, deluded with the hope that it would be taken into consideration and they would escape the severe penalty. He was determined to put a stop to that sort of thing; if Read had not pleaded guilty no doubt some extenuating circumstance would have come up during the trial and he would have saved his life.

There, if ever, spoke the 'human devil' in a black cap!

I find another case of a sentence of transportation for life on a youth of eighteen, named Edward Baker, for stealing a pocket-handkerchief. Had he pleaded guilty it might have been worse for him.

At the Salisbury Spring Assizes, 1830, Mr Justice Gazalee, addressing the grand jury, said that none of the crimes appeared to be marked with circumstances of great moral turpitude. The prisoners numbered 130; he passed sentence of death on twenty-nine, life transportations on five, fourteen years on five, seven years on eleven, and various terms of hard labour on the others.

The severity of the magistrates at the quarter-sessions was equally revolting. I notice in one case, where the leading magistrate on the bench was a great local magnate, an M.P. for Salisbury, etc., a poor fellow with the unfortunate name of Moses Snook was charged with stealing a plank ten feet long, the property of the aforesaid local magnate, M.P. etc., and sentenced to fourteen years transportation. Sentenced by the man who owned the plank, worth perhaps a shilling or two!

W.H. Hudson
*A Shepherd's Life* (1910)

# Parted For Ever

Mrs Cadby also remembers her parents' account of seeing a local boy, convicted of sheep-stealing, driven off in a wagon towards Halesworth on the first stage of the terrible journey to Botany Bay. (Many of the convicts used to die owing to the vile conditions on board the convict ships). His mother, a tall gaunt woman, had come to say good-bye though she was not allowed in the wagon. As the constable pulled him away she said, 'When you get to Australia, look at the moon when that's full, and I will too. Then we'll know we're looking at the same moon.'

The wagon started, the woman striding behind in silence. Mother and son knew they would never meet again.

*Westleton*, edited by Alan Ivimey
(WEA Westleton Branch, 1968)

# A Picker

A capital story was told by a Bishop of Worcester, in connection with the efforts of the Church in that part of the country to alleviate the lot of the hop-pickers, who flock into Worcestershire in September by the thousand. One of the mission workers, who had gone down to the hopyards, met a dilapidated individual in a country lane, who said he was 'a picker.' Pressed for further particulars, the man responded: 'In the summer I picks peas and fruit; when autumn comes I pick hops; in the winter I picks pockets; and when I'm caught I picks oakum. I'm kept nice and warm during the cold months, and when the fine days come round once more I starts pea-picking again.'

Arthur H. Savory
*Grain and Chaff from an English Manor* (Blackwell, 1920)

# A Very Great Shame

It has been the custom in our neighbourhood, ever since I was a boy, that if a woman was cleaning turnips in a field she might take two or three, once or twice in a week. Farmers did not object, as a rule, and I have often seen women when turnip-cleaning put some into their aprons before the employer's face; it was an understood thing farmers have made such offers of turnips to me, and of course I have taken them; I no more thought of refusing them than I would have thought of refusing to put my week's wages in my pocket. After the act* came into operation the police set upon these women – respectable, honest, married women – searched them, brought them before the magistrate at Warwick, and charged them with stealing turnips. The police prosecuted and gave evidence, and the women were fined. It was a very great shame, and the village people were very bitter and sore about it.

Joseph Arch
*Joseph Arch, the story of his life, told by himself*
(Hutchinson, 1898)

* Poaching Prevention Act (1862).

# The Constable's Story

'Sir Robert he sent for me one day', the country constable related. 'And this time it wasn't rabbits. "Copperfield", says he, "I want you to find out who destroys the park wall all along the highway, pushing down the coping stones. I've had Maddocks, the mason, up to put them back over and over again." "Right, Sir", says I, and I stayed out all night. No one come. Next night I went again. Nothing doin' and me starving cold. Then 'bout three, footsteps. I lay still. Then I puts me 'ead up, Maddocks!'

G.M.L.T.
*The Countryman*, October 1935

# The Tramp

'Well, if you are curious, how would you like to hear of the murder I did twenty years ago? I tell it to everybody, and they don't seem to believe me, so I will tell it to you …

'I spent a night in the workhouse and when I got out in the afternoon I was so hungry that I could have eaten the master, if he hadn't been the ugliest fellow I ever saw, like a fancy potato. Walking didn't cure my appetite, and all that day and night I didn't have a bite. Perhaps I got a bit queer and I went on walking until I got near to Binoll in Wiltshire where I was born. That is a fine country. My old woman and I have slept in violets there many a time in April. When I got there early in the morning on the second day I thought I would go into a copse I knew and pick some bluebells there, partly for old remembrance sake and partly to make a penny or two in Swindon, but I didn't much care what. Well, as I was picking them – God! how everything did smell and I felt like a little boy, I was enjoying it so, and putting my hand into all the nests and feeling the warm eggs – Lord! what a fool I be – I thought I would go to sleep. There was such a nice bit of moon in the sky, with the rim of the cup of it uppermost, which means that it keeps the rain from falling, but if it is upside down it lets the water out and you may know it will rain. There was a regular old-fashioned English thrush saying: "Bit, bit, slingdirt, slingdirt, belcher, belcher, belcher," and I went on picking the flowers. All of a sudden I saw two fellows sitting just outside the wood with their backs to me. One of them was a big fellow and we passed the time of day and he said he had done a job lately and was not in a hurry to do any more. The other was a little white-faced man such as I can't away with, and he said he was looking for a job and trying to get his strength up a bit. The big fellow motioned to me, meaning that the other had got money about him; so I agreed, and nodded, and he stepped back and hit the little fellow a good blow on the head. I threw away the flowers and we dragged him into the wood. He had ten shillings on him and we took half each. He looked very bad, so the other fellow said: "We had better put him away," and I said: "Yes, he may be in awful pain, such a white-faced fellow as he is." So we knocked the life out of him, and the other fellow went off Marlborough way and I went into Swindon and had such a dinner as I hadn't had for weeks, rabbit and new potatoes and a bit of curry … Did you ever hear about that?

'Get on my mind? Why, I never meant the fellow any harm and I filled my belly.'

Edward Thomas
*The Heart of England* (Dent, 1906)

# An Affray

There had been a great deal of poaching before the affray took place, and finally it grew to horse-stealing: one night two valuable horses were taken from the home park. This naturally roused the indignation of the owner of the estate, who resolved to put a stop to it. Orders were given that if shots were heard in the woods the news should be at once transmitted to headquarters, no matter at what hour of the night.

One brilliant, moonlight night, frosty and clear, the gang came again. A messenger went to the house, and, as previously arranged, two separate parties set out to intercept the rascals. The head-keeper had one detachment, whose object it was to secure the main outlet from the wood towards the adjacent town

– to cut off retreat. The young squire had charge of the other, which, with the under-keeper as guide, was to work its way through the wood and drive the gang into the ambuscade. In the last party were six men and a mastiff dog; four of the men had guns, the gentleman only a stout cudgel.

They came upon the gang – or rather a part of it, for the poachers were somewhat scattered – in a 'drive' which ran between tall firs, and was deep in shadow. With a shout the four or five men in the 'drive', or green lane, slipped back behind the trees, and two fired, killing the mastiff dog on the spot and 'stinging' one man in the legs. Quick as they were, the under-keeper, to use his own words, 'got a squint of one fellow as I knowed; and I lets drive both barrels in among the firs. But, bless you! it were all over in such a minute that I can't hardly tell 'ee how it were. Our squire ran straight at 'em; but our men hung back, though they had their guns and he had nothing but a stick. I just seen him as the smoke rose, hitting at a fellow; and then, before I could step, I hears a crack, and the squire he was down on the sward. One of them beggars had come up behind, and swung his gun round and fetched him a purler on the back of his head. I picked him up, but he was as good as dead, to look at'; and in the confusion the poachers escaped.

Richard Jefferies
*The Gamekeeper at Home* (1878)

# Poaching by Candlelight

I have this from a man of seventy-five who started work on market gardens and farms around Southampton when he was six, and was driving a wagon of produce to market at two o'clock in the morning before he was ten: 'The keepers them days was very lively and it didn't do for 'em to catch you out with no nets nor no ferrets. Nets you can drop quick when they comes at you and not show, but it's not so easy getting rid of a ferret, specially when them keepers 'ad a dog as well as a gun. But the fishing folk around the Solent, they didn't need no ferrets to bolt their rabbits for 'em, see? They was a rough lot them days down that way. Fish six months and work on the farms six months. It's an old saying, fruit kills fish, for you can't sell fish no sense once there's fruit about. Well those men say they got to know a good bury when they was working on the farms. Next time they was down on the shore, they'd collect up one or two of them big old king crabs, that's what they'd do. King crabs it 'ad to be, and make a 'arness for 'em they would, that'd 'old one of them little candlesticks like you might 'ave on a birthday-cake. Take a candle that'd last ten or say fifteen minutes.

'Then they'd wait till a good dark night, when the keepers'd think a poacher couldn't see to work, and not windy weather neither mind, and along they'd go to that there bury they'd marked, and fix that 'arness on that big old king crab, and a long bit of string tied to him, and stand him out of the wind down the bury. Then they'd light that little candle on his back and give him a push, and that big old king crab'd go sideways down that bury, slow an' steady. Very steady sideways 'e'd go down that bury into the dark with the candle lighted on 'is back, and when the rabbits down that bury woke and saw that big old king crab coming down at 'em with that flaming candle on his back – bolt! You'd ought to see 'em bolt! Ten in one net I've counted myself. Then all the man had to do was collect up all them rabbits and pull back that old king crab and take off his harness and get along back home quick.

'There's ignorant people don't believe that when I tell 'em; but true as I stand here, I've seen it with these two eyes.'

P. Fforde
*The Countryman*

# The Poacher

Years ago a new policeman was appointed at Wickhambrook and he announced that he was going to put a stop to poaching. Whereupon my poaching employee announced in the inn that he would shoot dead anyone who interfered with him. Of course, he did not seriously mean to do this. Crimes of violence are rare in Suffolk, partly because of the nature of the people and partly because there are very few southern Irish or eastern Europeans to be found living here. The poacher had hoped to frighten the policeman off; but it did not frighten him.

So, a little while later, in the dusk of the evening, the policeman caught the poacher on a footpath with a sack on his back which bulged suspiciously. He demanded to look in the sack. The poacher protested his innocence but finally reluctantly let the policeman look inside. What he found were several loaves of bread, so placed that they looked like the shape of pheasants. The poacher then went to the inn and spread the story and the policeman was held up to ridicule. This successfully curbed the policeman's ambition to stop all poaching in his district. This poacher had in fact learnt the most effective way of dealing with officials of all kinds. He held the policeman up to ridicule. You can abuse an Englishman as much as you like and he just smiles; you can argue with an Englishman as much as you like and he remains unconvinced. But if you hold him up to ridicule, the victory is yours.

Justin and Edith Brooke
*Suffolk Prospect* (1963)

# Interview with a Poacher

Many years ago I had an interview with a poacher, which, though it was very brief, and not a word was spoken, produced a great excitement, a memorable alternation of despair and victory. Walking with my gun by the side of a brook which ran through my property, in search of the wild duck, which sometimes came in the winter from the frozen lakes, in the neighbourhood, and from the Trent, to our running stream, I had reached a point where it was crossed by a bridge and a public road. On this road, to my right, and but a few yards from the bridge, stood a man, who also carried a gun, and who, my keeper informed me, was a notorious poacher. The words had only just passed his lips when a fine mallard rose in front of us and flew towards the bridge. I suppose that I was nervous in such an august presence, but whatever was the cause, I fired and missed! The mallard was now an easy shot for the poacher, when, as he deliberately raised his gun, I pulled the trigger of my second barrel, and the bird fell dead at his feet. I shall never forget the dissolving view on the keeper's countenance, from the scowl of disgust to the grin of delight when he went to fetch the drake!

*The Memories of Dean Hole* (Nelson, *c.* 1900)

# A Tidy Drop

Last in this very brief review of Forest celebrities is one who shall be nameless, but who is well known in the village where, at the time of writing he still lives. In the records of the local magistrates' court his name appears as an honest and fearless witness; a man who could be relied upon to speak his mind. It happened that he had been called by the prosecution in a claim for damage caused by rabbits. The defence sought to undermine his reliability, and the cross-examination went something like this:

'I understand, my man, that you are not averse to a glass of beer?'

'That's right, I'm none the worse for a glass or two.'

'It is even suggested that you drink a considerable quantity.'

'Ah, I do that, when I can get 'un.'

'Now, can you tell the Court how much you would drink in a day?'

'In a day!' – with a note of hopeless alarm.

'Well, shall we say in an evening?'

'Oh, of a evening. That's more like. Well, of a evening I sometimes have me six or eight quarts. But, (in a tone of joyful recollection) sometimes I have a tidy drop.'

I have never dared to ask the outcome of the case. The thought of such honesty going unrewarded would be more than I could bear.

F. W. Baty
*The Forest of Dean* (1952)

# Sport

# At the Tother End

'Moreton-in-the-Marsh be a desperate place for cricket; they does the job proper there, a mowed ground, a painted pavilion, all on 'em playing in white trousers and little bwoy caps and all. On Saturday they was a-playing a village team from up on they hills – Longborough – as hadn't got all the tackle like Moreton men, some of 'em in corduroys even, and there was only one pair of pads for the whole 'leven of 'em, and they was odd 'uns; so the batsmen could only wear one each. Well, it come their turn to bat against the Moreton men. "Bill," one of 'em said to tother, "you've got your pad on the wrong leg." "Have I?" says Bill. "Then you best let 'im bowl at you and I'll go in at the tother end!" '

H.J. Massingham
*Shepherd's Country* (1938)

# Village Cricket

Our village, being a relatively poor one, was later than some in playing organised cricket. There was no halfday holiday on Saturdays sixty years ago for land workers.

On the 28th January, 1907, a meeting was held in the school, I have the minutes in front of me now. The Reverend Hornsby, the curate, was appointed captain and a set of rules was drawn up. The first six rules were quite ordinary and could have applied to any cricket club, but rule number seven was different. This rule stated that the committee reserved the right to dismiss any member for disorderly or bad conduct on the ground.

The vice-captain appointed was Mr Arthur Jackson, a small farmer whose holding was on the hill. The cricket ground belonged to Mr Fred Beasley, a large farmer who let the ground to the club for one pound per year.

The first match was fixed against Norton and Lenchwick on the 1st May, 1907. The pavilion in the Broadenham was an old railway carriage and things looked set for a good season. But at a general meeting held on the 15th August, 1907, about six months after the formation of the club, a letter was read by the secretary from Mr Fred Beasley giving notice to the club that he refused to let one of the members, namely Arthur Jackson, play in any other match that season on his ground owing to some grievance between themselves. The trouble was that Mr Jackson's cattle had broken through the fence into Mr Beasley's mowing grass and the two men had fallen out. The chairman explained that it was the duty of the members to decide whether Mr Jackson had broken any of the club's rules and what steps they should take in the matter. The meeting came to a most unusual decision. They decided by a majority of seven votes that Arthur Jackson had broken rule number seven and that he was barred from playing again that season. Mr Fred Beasley then went on renting the ground to the club. A stormy year for the first year of a village team! How Arthur Jackson broke rule number seven by disorderly conduct on the field, when what really happened was that he had had words with Fred Beasley over his cattle breaking through into some mowing grass a mile away from the cricket pitch, no one can explain.

Next year, Arthur Jackson, who had been dismissed from the Ashton Cricket Club, started with Alf Pickford, the younger Alf Pickford and a few more who took Jackson's part, in what became known as the United Cricket Club. The new club played in a field of Alf Pickford's known as the New Piece. These two teams ran 'at loggeryuds', as Charlie Bradfield said, for three years. When a meeting was held in the school on 10th May, 1910, Mr James Longfield was in the chair. He had recently come to live in the village and said the purpose of the meeting was to try and bring the two committees together and all would work together as one club. After a lengthy discussion the United Club agreed to throw in their lot with the Ashton Club, leaving representatives of both clubs on the committee.

Young Alf Pickford objected to serving on the committee and his father proposed, and it was carried, that he should be fined one guinea. It was decided that night that if any disputes arose in the club between members at the committee meeting or in any other way all disputes should be settled by the president and chairman, Mr James Longland. Mr Longland agreed to give a bat to the player with the best average. After this troublesome start the club went from strength to strength and reached its heyday in the twenties when Mr Edgar Longland, the son of the president, was captain and with the aid of an excellent groundsman produced a wicket near the station which was the talk of the district. High scores were commonplace; the outfield was as good as the square. Old-time umpires were a race apart and Lofty Summers was no exception. Ashton were playing Dumbleton and the last pair were batting for the visitors when Harry Shakespeare, Ashton's fast bowler, bowled a yorker. The Dumbleton batsman, playing with his bat and pad close together, edged the ball with his bat on to his pad. Lofty shouted, 'Out!' 'How can he be out?' the Ashton captain said. 'There's been no appeal and he played the ball with his bat.' Lofty was unmoved. 'The ball hit him on the leg and anyroad I wants my tay and he's out.' Whether this affected the result of the match, I can't say, but it was an unusual decision. A visiting team from the other side of the hill were playing on our home ground and their umpire with his white smock and his pipe going appeared to be watching the game, but one appeal brought the reply, 'Not out, but if it occurs again it will be, to an appeal for l.b.w.'

Edgar Longland, apart from being a keen cricketer and a good sport (he encouraged us boys), was a bit of a wag and he wanted a blacksmith to work on his farm to shoe and do repairs. He put an advertisement in the local paper for a blacksmith, preferably one who could play cricket. Whether Caleb Batchelor had ever handled a cricket bat before is a thing no one will ever know, but he was a useful blacksmith and turned out for the team on the Saturday. I shall never forget him. He wore white flannels but with broad braces and a leather belt with a huge brass buckle. His arms were like legs of mutton, well tattooed, and as he waddled out to bat at about number eight the locals were wondering how he would shape. I think the team was Alcester and Ragley, one of the best teams we played. Caleb took centre for the first ball from their fast bowler. He ran up the pitch, turned a well pitched ball on the off into a full toss and sent it as if he was hitting the anvil to the square leg boundary. His sledge hammer strokes produced the runs and the better the ball, the harder he thumped it. Straight drives went to long on and agricultural strokes to leg. After he had made fifty he was caught out on the square leg boundary, but he had played himself into the team. I suppose that after a day swinging a sledge hammer this was child's play for Caleb. The day he made history in our village was when he hit a six over the scoring hut; it landed at Gloucester twenty miles away. You see the ball landed in an open railway truck as a goods train passed through the station and was found when the train stopped at Gloucester.

Fred Archer
*The Distant Scene* (1967)

# It Don't Matter

The village umpire having given a man out, a crowd surrounds him, some disputing his ruling, others supporting him, and all noisy. Presently the batsman saunters up and says, 'Well, it don't much matter because I ain't agoin' out.'

*The Countryman*, October 1935

# Beware of Clergymen

Yesterday we were shooting in Tindale Wood, a great covert of about 120 acres, which even now, however, is very thick with leaf, some of the undergrowth being almost as green as though we were still in the month of June. This quantity of foliage, even if one can see the creatures, makes hare and rabbit shooting rather dangerous, as it is difficult to know when the beaters are close at hand. However, nobody was shot, perhaps because we had no clergymen among the party. Great as is my respect for the clergy, although there are exceptions (I myself know one), I confess that I am not fond of going out shooting with them, since on these occasions they are apt to display too active a trust in a watching Providence. When I was a young fellow there lived in our neighbourhood a retired naval chaplain, who in private life was a most delightful old gentleman, but who when armed with a gun became a perfect terror. On one occasion I was joining a party of shooters who were advancing up a turnip field, and, seeing among them my reverend friend, I was particularly careful to show myself and call out to him. When he arrived within about twenty yards of me, however, a partridge rose at his feet and flew straight past me, whereon, without the slightest hesitation, he sent the contents first of one barrel and then of the other slap into the fence within about a foot of my face.

'Mr B.! Mr. B!' I exclaimed reproachfully, 'You very nearly shot me dead.'

'Oh,' he grunted in answer, 'shouldn't have been there, you know; shouldn't have been there!'

On another occasion the same dear old gentleman nearly blew the middle out of one of my brothers, in fact he only escaped the charge by doubling himself up with a wonderful rapidity. After that experience we dared not ask him to shoot any more. This gave him great offence, as he believed that the omission was due to personal reasons. It is very difficult to make the dangerous man understand what a thing of fear he is to all his neighbours.

Here is a further reminiscence of a parsonic sportsman. The parson and another friend entered the top of a long covert with a view to walking down it in line and shooting rabbits while I stood at the bottom waiting for pheasants. There were a good many shots fired in the covert, varied by occasional shouts, and at last my friend staggered out at the end looking very hot and flustered.

'You had some shooting there,' I said.

'Shooting?' he answered in a fury. 'That infernal parson had the shooting. He has been firing at my legs all down the grove, and I've been jumping the shot.'

Afterwards this reverend gentleman very nearly slew me also in mopping up a low pheasant, at which no man ought to have fired.

Once, too, I knew another clergyman who went out ferreting with a companion and, turning suddenly, aimed his gun at that unfortunate's boot and – hit it. When remonstrated with he said that he thought it was a black rabbit. However, he was only a curate, from whom caution could scarcely be expected.

H. Rider Haggard
*A Farmer's Year*, November 1898

# A Smoke

And that goes back to when I was a boy, when there was money about. We boys used to go beating. They used to give us cider, good strong stuff that'd burn the name off a tombstone, and a bit of cheese and fat pork and we'd be at it all day. They were proper shoots then, all the daylight long. Of course some of the gentlemen couldn't carry the cider, they weren't used to stuff like that, you see. I remember one day there hadn't been many rabbits about, but me and another fellow got one and stuck it against a tree with a cigarette in his mouth. Just for a joke like, for a laugh. Then after his lunch and a good drop of cider, one gentleman came along, saw this rabbit, put up his gun sharp and then down with it, and he shook his head and he said: 'No,' he said, 'I won't shoot you, I like a smoke myself.'

J. Munday, Kent
BBC *Country Magazine*

# The Fox-Diviner

About eight years ago I put two terriers to ground in an earth under a crop of oats. One, a Lakeland, was mute and the other, a Russell-type terrier, stopped sounding after a few minutes. We did not like to damage the crop as the owner was absent, and were talking it over when I saw a neighbouring farmer cut a forked stick out of the hedge and start walking over the earth.

Each time he came to a certain spot in the field the stick twisted in his hands. When I held his wrists I could feel a tremor when he reached the spot. I tried to use the stick but there was no reaction. We dug down and got each terrier fast in a fox cub, which accounted for the silence of the sounder.

The incident was witnessed by the local M.O.H. and the vet. The farmer concerned is a well-known water diviner.

Henry J. Carr
*The Field*

# Stag Hunt

One further story of red deer remains, relating to an ancestor of mine who dates from the mid-nineteenth century. He was Mr Tom Nevill of Chilland House, Chilland, near Winchester, who was famous for his pack of bloodhounds with which he used to hunt a carted stag. The nucleus of this pack was obtained from keepers in the New Forest and was almost entirely black in colour with tan on their legs and a tan spot over each eye. Although this type of hound became much lighter in build and faster in later years, he maintained their distinctive colour until his death. About the year 1854 he had an old red deer by name of Monarch which he hunted for several seasons. When he was released from the cart the old stag would be given a few minutes' grace before the pack was laid on. He would then run for as long as he wished, then turn and bay at the pack until Mr Nevill rode up. Then followed a spectacle which the followers had almost foundered their horses to witness. The pack was called off, the Master addressed the stag by name, old Monarch came up to him and amid the applause of the 'field' trotted home alongside Mr Nevill's horse.

J.A.N. Fitt
*The Bob Man* (Moonraker Press, 1977)

# The Sack

I have heard Percy Williams say that there was a certain district, not far from Market Harborough, which no horse could negotiate. His name recalls my excursive thoughts to the Rufford, of which he was for many years the successful Master. He was a thorough sportsman, lived at the kennels, like the old tradesmen over their shops, turned out his men, hounds and horses in excellent order, and was always punctual. Sometimes too punctual, as when, in the days of cub-hunting, he appeared very early on a September morning in a distant part of the hunt, and not finding a fox in the first wood that he tried, said to a boy waiting outside, 'Well, my lad, and where are all these foxes of which I have heard so much?' 'Oh, if you please, sir,' replied the guileless youth, 'fayther hasn't brought him yet.' The keeper had a bagman in reserve to deceive his master, whose orders to preserve foxes he had disobeyed, and his delay in producing him lost him his situation – his employer gave him the sack.

*The Memories of Dean Hole* (Nelson, *c.* 1900)

# Courtship and Marriage

# Stocky Hill

Stocky Hill, as he was called in the village, was Jasper's elder brother and lived in a cottage next door. He was a batchelor then, a terrific worker able to cut an acre of wheat in a day with the two hooks, but he was more noted for his digging the heavy clay soil of the village. A chain or four hundred and eighty four square yards with an Evesham Two Tine or two-prong digger didn't come amiss to him. Job Barley, our cowman, used to describe him as a stomachful. He didn't mean Stocky was awkward, but that he could not give in or give up a job. There was nothing one would notice about his appearance in the late twenties. Wearing a black kind of beaver hat, cord waistcoat and cord trousers, both of washed-out fawn, he was upright, broad-shouldered, a man who looked full of work yet. He was named Stocky for obvious reasons, Jasper, his brother, being head and shoulders taller.

He had a face which fairly bristled with whiskers, the beard kept fairly short. He smoked a pipe, usually a clay one, and the pleasant scent of Red Bell Shag on a frosty morning as he passed our house was so in keeping with the countryside, the birds, the flowers, and between the high-banked hedges of our lane it lingered in a blue-grey cloud. Like Stocky, a part of nature itself.

Despite the mature, rugged look of this village Hampden he started courting at about sixty-five a servant girl of doubtful age from Cheltenham. Stocky used to take her back towards the big house in Cheltenham where she worked, walking with her to the Farmers Arms nearly at Bishops Cleeve. She pushed her bike and these Sunday Nights Stocky walked about fifteen miles. In his own words he said, when he kissed her goodnight, 'That rattled just like a whip a-smacking!' On her days off Stocky and Ada did a part of their courting down the snaky, wandering lane known as Back Lane or Gipsies Lane.

Stocky was a man of few words. No wonder he had started courting very late in life and he had to learn. 'Why doesn't say

135

summat?' Ada said one night. (The boys had followed them to catch every word.) 'What be I to say?' said Stocky. 'Why doesn't say as you loves me?' 'So I do,' said Stocky. Ada followed up with, 'Don't the stars shine bright tonight?' 'Oi, they do,' replied Stocky.

This unusual courtship went on for some time and they thought of marriage. Stocky spoke to the vicar, who asked him the name of the lucky girl. 'Ada,' said Stocky. The vicar said, 'I know that. What I want to know is her surname.' 'Lor bless the fella I couldn't tell tha. I allus calls her darling,' Stocky said in a rather superior tone. The vicar sorted things out and then trouble started. The Hill family thought it was a very unsatisfactory union and refused to have anything more to do with Stocky Hill. The old chap was furious, brought his bag of sixty golden sovereigns down to the village cross and, with the youths egging him on, said he had decided to broadcast his money there and then and throw it to anyone, then go and jump into the moat. 'Go on Stocky, show um you means business,' they told him, but he put his money back in his inside poacher's pocket of his Derby tweed jacket, and walked up to the moat, the lads egging him on and saying, 'Show um you means business.'

There was no broadcasting of Stocky's sovereigns and he didn't jump in the moat but the following Sunday morning in our village church Edward Hill and Ada Styles were asked in church for the first time. Stocky was persuaded to go and when his name was read out he said in a loud stage whisper, 'Lors, that made I sweat,' mopping his brow with a clean red and white spotted handkerchief.

The wedding day arrived but Stocky was not an easy man to marry. When the vicar popped the question he answered 'Yes' instead of 'I will.' 'You must say "I will", Mr Hill,' the vicar insisted, and Stocky came out with 'All right then, if that's it, I will.'

At the lichgate at the bottom of the churchyard and at the village cross quite a handful of people had gathered to wish this odd couple well. But Stocky and Ada were signing the register and Milly Bosworth was playing suitable pieces on the organ. Stocky could not sign his name, only mark a cross. Stocky and Ada did not come out of the church door, through the porch and down the churchyard. 'Oh no, my boy,' as Stocky told me later. 'I knowed they was a-waiting for us down in that lichgate with their rice and their 'fetti so me and the missis came out of the back vestry door and took the footpath across the field to the cottage.' The vicar asked Stocky about a honeymoon. Stocky said, 'Bless the fellow. We've already had that on Fuzz Hill.'

After the wedding they settled down happily but Stocky was always in evidence if there was an election, firmly believing that things didn't go off as they should if there was no fighting, and he would try and start something of the sort for old time's sake, remembering the rowdy elections of his youth.

Fred Archer
*The Distant Scene* (1967)

# A Wedding Present

Sydney B —, a small farmer and cider maker had a reputation for being parsimonious. He would have described himself as 'careful', but his neighbours said he was mean, 'near', or 'tight', and that he had 'a tidy little packet tucked away'. However, when his nephew Fred was about to be married he obviously felt that he could not let the occasion pass without making some avuncular token.

On the eve of the wedding he went to see his nephew. 'Well, Fred,' he said, 'I hear you be gettin' wed tomorrow.' Fred nodded and his uncle paused a while before saying, 'I'm afraid I can't afford to buy a present for you.' Then, bringing his hand from behind his back, Sydney B — said, 'But here's a lovely bunch of beetroot for you.'

Humphrey Phelps

# Marrying to Oblige in the 1930s

The batchelor farmer, if he has no woman relative to look after his farmhouse, employs a housekeeper and propinquity often has its expected result, whether this is accompanied with a marriage ceremony or not. A new rector was appointed to a

West Suffolk living and he found to his dismay that one of his most respected parishioners and a regular attendant in church was living in sin, as they say, with his housekeeper. Of course he had to take action and the farmer in question related to Dr. Wilkin what occurred:

'The Reverend kept crazing us to get married. I say: 'Why should we? We get along very comfortable' – but he go on and on, fairly mobbing me; so we put on our best clothes and go to church; and he say, 'Wilt thou take this woman to be thy wedded wife?' and I say, 'Course I will; I comed a-purpose'; then he say, 'If you don't treat this ceremony with proper respect, I shan't marry you;' and I say, 'I only come here to oblige you and I can go away' – then he marry us – quick and sharp!'

Justin and Edith Brooke
*Suffolk Prospect* (1963)

# Married Himself

An odd circumstance happened at Shepton Mallet about a fortnight since. Mr. F —, the Curate of that place, published the Banns of Marriage of himself for three Sundays, the third time and after the second Lesson he asked (aloud) if the Rector was present, or whether he had appointed a Deputy to marry him. On being answered in the Negative, he said he should perform the ceremony himself, which he did in the presence of the Congregation, and said the Rector must answer to the Bishop.

*Drewry's Derby Mercury*
September 1787

# The Wedding

I started to play the first voluntary, a sickly piece by a minor nineteenth century German composer. At least it served to quieten the mob. Before it came to an end on a soft diapason the vicar had banged into the vestry and was robing. I peeped over the top of the organ loft. The bridegroom had not arrived. Neither had he appeared by a quarter to one. A terrible fear came over me that Perce had jilted her at the last minute. By ten to one I had played three of my repertoire of four pieces and only had Mendelssohn's Wedding March left. (This in a simplified version.) And I couldn't give them that yet. So I began to regale them with a series of hymns, each ornamented with my best twiddly bits. I don't know what they made of 'Lo, He comes with Clouds Descending' followed by 'Glorious Things of Thee are Spoken.' The imp in me wanted to play 'Fierce Raged the Tempest o'er the Deep' but I restrained myself in time. The Vicar was fidgeting by the vestry door; I knew he would soon be in a vile temper.

Then when I was enjoying myself, improving on 'The Voice That Breathed O'er Eden', Perce and his best man walked in, rather unsteadily, I thought, up the central aisle. I wondered if they had been fortifying themselves. Perce had a glazed look and didn't seem to be with us. But who, in the name of fortune, had told him to wear brown plus fours and brown patent leather shoes? I could hear laughter gently ripping around the church. I went on playing. Bob whispered from the back of the organ, "Ere go easy, I'm puffed.' But I just had to go on, hymns, variations, everything I knew, except of course the Wedding March. I could see Perce just below me sitting bolt upright in his pew. Then, at twenty-five past one, when several of the congregation had already left, there was a flutter at the bottom of the church, and everybody rose, that is, all but 'Silly' Ted. Unfortunately, I lost my head and started to play the Wedding March as Gladys entered on her father's arm. Hot with confusion, I watched them, out of the corner of my eye, moving very slowly up the church. Philip was wearing a loud check suit, with a fancy spotted waistcoat, an enormous yellow cravat – and spats. His bowler hat was clutched tightly to his paunch. He looked like an old fashioned bookie going to a party. But as long as I live I shall never forget the sight of Gladys. She was a symphony in purple. And it was a purple of so violent a hue that she could have passed for a comic Roman empress in fancy dress. Her frock was purple, her shoes were purple, her veil was purple, her purple toque was embellished with knots of artificial Parma violets. She carried a bunch of pink carnations. As they got nearer, it became obvious to me that they had fortified themselves, too. Not that they were unsteady. Only splendid and glorious. Gladys was a great purple ship in full sail. She and her smiling father walked up to the waiting Vicar who was looking as black as thunder. There were no bridesmaids. Someone pushed Perce into his proper place where he stood, spellbound, and in utter dejection. But, bless me, when Gladys and her father had got as far as the choir steps, they did not stop there, but turned in grandeur down the north aisle. The congregation were still standing. Even 'Silly' Ted had got on a seat and was peering over the tops of shoulders. I went on playing with every stop out. Gladys and her father got to the bottom of the church. Now, I thought, it will all come right. But, dear me, no. They then made for the south aisle and paraded up that. By the time the ridiculous perambulations had finished, they had been right round the church. But at last they were by Percy's side and the service began. I was sweating like a pig.

Then Percy suddenly began hiccuping. The best man could not find the ring and had to fumble in all his pockets for it. When at last he discovered it he further enlivened the proceedings by turning round, holding it on high and saying, 'I got 'un. I knew I had 'un somewhere.' When asked if she would take Percy to be her lawful wedded husband, Gladys convulsed us by saying, 'Of course.' 'Just say "I will"', barked the Vicar. Percy went on hiccuping.

Somehow or other they got to the end of it. I cannot remember all the details. But the Vicar preached no sermon and did not appear again. As they were going into the vestry to sign the register, a christening party turned up at the bottom of the church and sat in the seats near the font. And when I struck up the Wedding March again, the baby went into competition with me. Perce, hanging on to his wife's arm, looked more miserable than ever. As they walked past the baby Percy gave it a very old-fashioned look.

Leonard Clark
*A Fool in the Forest* (1965)

# Labour in Vain

The sign which stood there now was of a cherry tree. Our farmhouse had become 'The Cherry Tree Inn'. I went inside and there I found a farmer, who might have once been a neighbour of my own, telling a story of his start many years ago on a small farm as a just-married man. The first thing they did together, bride and bridegroom of a night, was to drill five acres with carrot seed. He drove the horses while she went behind the drill. He showed her how to cut off the flow of seed when they turned at the headland, by pushing down a lever, and then to release it again when they started a new journey across the seed-bed.

They finished the job and came home to a late dinner. When they came into the yard, he raised the lid of the seedbox. There was as much carrot seed in it as there had been when they began the job. His wife had depressed the lever when she should have raised it, and vice versa. They had been all over that five acres and sown hardly one tiny seed. She dished out the dinner happily, and he sat down to it with her, and he said not a word.

Next day he sent her off to market for something, and while she was gone he went out and drilled the whole field again by himself.

'Mind you, if she made that mistake today I should tell her about it quick enough,' he laughed.

Adrian Bell
*My Own Master* (1961)

# Wife For Sale

Yesterday forenoon, a disgraceful exhibition, the attempted sale of a wife, took place in front of a beer-house at Sheer Bridge, Little Horton, near Bradford. The fellow who offered his wife, Martha, for sale was Hartley Thompson. She was said to be a person of prepossessing appearance. The sale had been duly announced by the bellman. A large crowd had assembled. The wife, it is said, appeared before the crowd with a halter, adorned with ribbons, round her neck. The sale, however, was not completed; the reason for this being that some disturbance was created by a crowd from a neighbouring factory, and the person to whom it was intended to sell the wife (Ike Duncan) was detained at his work beyond the time. The couple, though not long wedded, have led a very unhappy life, and it is said they and their friends were so egregiously ignorant as to believe that they would secure their own legal separation by such an absurd course as this – a public sale.

*Manchester Guardian*
23 November 1858

## Buying a Daughter

Queer things happen down in the West Country, but one of the most singular is reported this week by the Weston Mercury. An action was brought in the Wincanton County Court by a baker, to recover from a Mrs Newport, the balance of an account for bread supplied to her by the plaintiff. His Honour: Is defendant a widow? Plaintiff: Yes, sir. Her husband went clean away a long time ago. His Honour: What do you mean? Is he dead, or has he merely left her? Plaintiff: Why, your Honour, they couldn't agree so he took her to Shepton Market and sold her. His Honour: How does defendant get her living? Plaintiff: Her father was at Shepton when she was sold, and he gave her husband £500 for her, and offered to allow her 10s. a week, which she has received ever since. His Honour then made an order for 10s. a month.

*Lincolnshire Chronicle*
9 April 1869

## Suffolk Story

The old doctor, Dr. Wilkin, told me that fifty years ago about a third of the births were illegitimate; the position is now very different, but the doctor attributed this to increased knowledge, rather than a higher standard of morality. The birth of an illegitimate child seems to have no effect on the future marriage prospects of the girl, and it is a common thing for the eldest child of a family to be markedly different from the rest of the children.

One of the Suffolk stories is this. A young man was going out with a girl, when his father drew him aside and said: 'You mustn't court that girl – she's my daughter.' The next girl he courted, the same result occurred; but when it happened a third time, he went off to his mother in a fury and said to her: 'You didn't ought to have let father carry on so' – to which she replied: 'Don't you take no heed of what he say, he ain't your father.'

Justin and Edith Brooke
*A Suffolk Prospect* (1963)

# Moses Found

The incident I am going to relate occurred about 1815 or perhaps two or three years later. The border of one of the deer walks was at a spot known as Three Downs Place, two miles and a half from Winterbourne Bishop. Here in a hollow of the downs there was an extensive wood, and just within the wood a large stone house, said to be centuries old but long pulled down called Rollston House, in which the head-keeper lived with the under-keepers. He had a wife but no children, and was a middle-aged, thick set, very dark man, powerful and vigilant, a 'terrable' hater and persecutor of poachers, feared and hated by them in turn, and his name was Harbutt.

It happened that one morning, when he had unbarred the front door to go out, he found a great difficulty in opening it, caused by a heavy object having been fastened to the door-handle. It proved to be a basket or box, in which a well-nourished, nice-looking boy baby was sleeping, well wrapped up and covered with a cloth. On the cloth a scrap of paper was pinned with the following lines written on it:

Take me in and treat me well
For in this house my father dwell.

Harbutt read the lines and didn't even smile at the grammar, on the contrary, he appeared very much upset, and was still standing holding the paper, staring stupidly at it, when his wife came on the scene. 'What be this?' she exclaimed, and looked first at the paper then at him, then at the rosy child fast asleep in its cradle; and instantly, with a great cry, she fell on it and snatched it up in her arms, and holding it clasped to her bosom, began lavishing caresses and endearing expressions on it, tears of rapture in her eyes! Not one word of inquiry or bitter, jealous reproach – all that part of her was swallowed up and annihilated in the joy of a woman who had been denied a child of her own to love and nourish and worship. And now one had come to her and it mattered little how. Two or three days later the infant was baptised at the village church with the quaint name of Moses Found.

W.H. Hudson
*A Shepherd's Life* (1910)

# Friday, 7 June 1811

I mounted on my horse after breakfast to ride to Stowgurcy to my Old Friend Mr Davis. He was at home but engaged to dine with Mr Acland so I could not stay with him long. He was busy papering his Sitting Parlour and Stockham one of the Jurymen on the woman who drowned herself was there. He says she was drunk when she did it, had a quarrel before with her Husband but he was not to blame in this matter nor aware of her intentions. She came into the house, put her cloak and hat on a nail and without saying a word went to the Well and threw herself down. It was forty feet deep and had twenty of water in it. The man went down after her at the Peril of his life, fastened her by a rope to the bucket. She when brought near the summit fell off and he went down again and brought her up by the assistance of men coming from Stowgurcy. He and his wife were large corpulent people and with the water in their clothes weighed little less than five hundred pounds and all this was brought up by the strength of a small rope.

Revd William Holland
*Paupers and Pig Killers* (1984)

# Superstition, the Supernatural and Other Strange Stories

# The Oak Gives up its Secret

Lately the necessity arose of cutting down some oaks on land of which I was in charge. No sooner had we cut off a limb from one tree than its balance was disturbed, and it split open with a groan from crown to foot. A hollow was disclosed where, to our amazement, staring at us from the cavity, stood the skeleton of a man in rusty armour. He was resting a little above ground level, knee deep in rotten wood and chips, which pigeons or squirrels had showered down from the opening above, chin on chest, hands on a mouldering sword. As we looked the sword broke and he dropped on his knees and crumbled almost to nothing. There was not much of him worth collecting; his bones were like dust; his mail like rusty red tissue paper. All we could guess was that he had had some good reason for a hurried hiding place, that he had come down the old road, and noticing the oaks, scrambled up the one we had felled and down into the inviting hollow within. He never thought of how he was going to get out, and, perhaps wounded, died of starvation.

E.L.A.
*The Countryman*, October 1935

# Sold to the Devil

There was one remarkable and deplorable thing about the old man, and that was his almost incredible superstitions; he had sold himself to the devil, and the compact was sealed for ever and ever. It was absolutely useless to attempt to reason with him on the point, or to show the impossibility of such a thing; it had not the slightest effect, he had sold himself to 'old Nick', and there was an end of it. How did it happen? Ah! that I could never tell. I often questioned the old man to know how the bargain was conducted, but he would never tell me that; he simply declared that he 'selled himself to Old Nick out in Maaster Pingedar's (Pinnegar's) ground, by the canal yander', when he was a young fellow. Oftentimes I tried to correct him from the error, and taught him to pray, and to think of Christ, Who came to save the world from sin, but he always burst out into piteous tears, sobbing like a child, and saying: ''Tis all right for t'other people, but nat vor I. Chent no good vor I. Old Nick got I right anough. He's allus along wi' ma, awaitin' vor ma, a swerin' and blerin' against God Almighty, he won never let ma aloan no more.' And this delusion he continued in right up to the end, for, though many came to see him, clergy and others, and prayed no end of times, it made no difference; he was fully persuaded that he was bound to the Evil One, nothing could shake his belief in that.

Alfred Williams
*A Wiltshire Village* (1912)

# The Devil Again

All he kep' on about was the devil. The devil kep' comin' and botherin' of'n. 'Tis a bad job. I s'pose he went right into it – studyin' about these here places nobody ever bin to an' come back again to tell we. Nobody don't know nothin' about it. 'Ten't as if they come back to tell ye. There's my father what bin dead this forty year. What a crool man he must be not to've come back in all that time, if he was able, an' tell me about it. That's what I said to Colonel Sadler. 'Oh,' he says, 'You better talk to the Vicar.' 'Vicar?' I says. 'He won't talk to me.' Besides, what do he know about it more'n anybody else?'

George Bourne
*Memoirs of a Surrey Labourer* (Duckworth, 1907)

# The Ravens' Cry

At the school this morning we were reading the verse 'Consider the ravens'. Robert Smith said that the night before Fannie

Lessiter of Sutton Lane died a raven was seen to sit upon the farmhouse roof and heard crying 'Corpse'.

John Vincent said that a man was sick at Derry Hill. Two ravens flew over the house crying 'Corpse, Corpse'. The man died the next day.

Miss Bland the schoolmistress has lost her brother a few days ago. One night at nine o'clock she was coming home from the village in the dusk when a young man passed her running swiftly without a sound and his feet did not touch the ground. She could not see his face, but she felt sure her brother was worse. A day or two afterwards she heard that on the day and at the hour when she saw the young man running her brother was struck for death.

Francis Kilvert, 26 May 1873
*Diaries*

# A Low State

It rained so hard last night that the water streamed through the roof of the Chancel. I read Prayers in the morning, and preached in the evening on the Seventh Commandment, 'Thou shalt not commit adultery,' and having discoursed on the heinousness of the now too prevalent crime, as destructive to all social comfort, I enlarged on the government of the thoughts.

We walked to Meadyates to call on Frapnell; he seems going rapidly. A woman of the name of Barr was sitting with him, who also had been ill, that is, in a low nervous way for some time.

On my entering into conversation with the poor man, he began to say that he had been brought to that state by the enemy; that, in short, Witchcraft had been practised upon him and that the woman who was sitting with him had been also a fellow sufferer. He told me a man had called upon them and shewn them a paper which said that others had been bewitched like them, and that they would not get well again unless they could undo the charm. I said I had read that paper, and it was a pack of the greatest nonsense I had ever seen, and that the person who gave it to him, and received money for thus deceiving him, might be very severely punished by the Magistrate.

I wished to make the poor man smile, and I succeeded by saying I had heard of a man who believed he was made of glass, and begged his friends not to come near for fear of breaking him; another had fancied himself a teapot; that his own mind might be so weakened by illness, and his nerves so relaxed that he might not be able to shake off such absurd fancies: that nothing could harm him if he believed only in God and if he said 'Get thee behind me, Satan,' when any evil ideas came into his mind he would sneak away like a coward.

John Skinner, 28 February 1830
*Journal of a Somerset Rector, 1803–1834* (1984)

# A Story of an Old Church

A curious story is told of this old church. It seems that the bell-ringers of Coaley once planned to steal its (Frocester's) solitary bell, and, going there one night after dark, they unhitched it and carried it halfway down the stairs of the tower to a landing, where they left it to go down into the churchyard for a rest and a smoke. When they returned to the landing to bring it down the last flight, however, they were astonished to discover a little old lady sitting on top of it. Now, they had seen no one enter the church, so that it puzzled them how she had contrived to get in without being observed. Anyway, they asked her if she would be kind enough to get off it, so that they could carry it away, but the old lady took no notice. Assuming that she must be deaf they started shouting at her. Still she took no notice, so they took hold of the bell, resolved to carry it and her together, for she looked very frail and light. Yet try as they would, they could not budge that bell an inch. They struggled and sweated to no purpose before it began to dawn on them that there must be something queer about the old lady – in fact, that she was not of this world at all. No sooner did the thought occur to them, than they left the bell, turned and ran down the stairs and across the fields to Coaley as fast as their legs could carry them.

Oddly enough, there is a local tradition that, when the bell was being cast, the lady who was giving it to the church threw her jewellery into the bell-metal. So it has been assumed that, to prevent her gift being stolen, it was this old lady's spirit which returned to Frocester and sat a-top the bell. It is certainly a fact that the bell was once found on a landing halfway down the stair after someone had apparently tried to steal it. And it is also a fact that George and I stood on that landing, and George (who knew nothing of the story) remarked: 'I say, there isn't half a rummy sort of feeling about this place.'

Lewis Wilshire
*The Vale of Berkeley* (1954)

# Strange

I was walking along a lane not far from the village – a lane I have walked along innumerable times, a lane I know as well as I know my own face in a shaving mirror. It was a beautiful afternoon and I had thought of spending a little time looking along the hedgerow banks, and maybe when I got down to the river of having a bathe. And so I was strolling along, smoking a pipe, and looking around me, and without a care to burden me.

The lane runs straight with but one bend to an old stone bridge over the river and then curves sharply away to run down the valley. I was about half-way to the bend when I again had that feeling, the knowledge, overwhelming and frightening, that I was not alone. I had not passed anyone on the land: I could not hear anything behind me. I knew these things. I knew that I was alone. I walked on for a few yards, telling myself not to be a fool. But the feeling persisted. Again I suddenly found myself sweating – and then I was running. I ran all the way to the bridge, and then I could run no further. There was no strength in my legs, and I felt weak and sick. I stopped on the bridge only because I could go no farther, and leaned against the parapet. And I knew that there was someone else on the bridge and I was frightened. And then round the bend from the valley came Joe, the carter, and two of the big shires. As soon as the horses saw me they began to rear and plunge, and one broke away and crashed through the hedge into the field by the river. My fear left me and I went across and helped Joe to quieten the mare, which was trembling, and then we both went across and caught the other, which was in a like condition.

Joe was at a loss to account for the behaviour of his horses, two very quiet animals that I knew well. He said he had never known them behave in such a way before. I asked him if he had seen anyone else on the road besides myself, and he looked surprised and said he had not. Then he said, 'You don't look too well, master. You do need a drink.'

There was some discussion of the incident at The Cricketers that evening. The general consensus of opinion was that one of the animals, or possibly both, had been stung. I do not know. I cannot explain any of it. I only know that I was not stung.

Brian Vesey-Fitzgerald
*A Country Chronicle* (1942)

# The Witch

The inns are full to-night, and more than the usual good feeling is evident among the ploughmen and farm hands, who beam at each other at the Red Lion, or engage in a long confidential chat on the year's happenings, the crops and harvest, lambs and foals, and draw comparisons between this and that time or season. Meanwhile Jonas and Dobbin, Shadrach and Angel seriously enumerate how many to their knowledge have met the Inglesham ghost, or tell of Betty the witch who lies buried on the roadside, three miles distant.

Old Betty was famed for many acts and was a sore trouble to the carters, cowmen, and shepherds round about, bringing the flocks and herds and pregnant mares under her powerful spell and working incalculable mischief upon all and sundry. At one time the lambs, calves and foals were stillborn. The gates and doors would fall off the hinges; the pumps would not draw water and the cream would not set in the broad pans. The cobbler could not work his wax while she was near, and half the people of the countryside fell sick, while she danced in the streets at midnight and spat upon hundreds of pins and young crows, as the villagers confidently believed.

Jonas, the ox-carter, had heard of a witch who had tampered

with a neighbour's pig and caused it to go mad in the sty. The owner of the animal, a farm labourer, was distressed at the occurrence and uncertain what to do. At length it occurred to him to bleed the pig. Accordingly he took the scissors and snipped a piece out of its ear, causing it to bleed profusely, when, behold! out of her house ran the old woman, grasping her fingers, which were streaming with blood. It appears that when the swine's ear was cut the witch, being in spirit within the pig, was also injured. The pig recovered but the villagers left the old woman alone, and she soon bled to death.

Alfred Williams
*Round About the Upper Thames* (Duckworth, 1922)

# Buttercup

Buttercup was a placid goodnatured cow; nothing ever upset her until that one afternoon. She came in to be milked as usual, went to her place in the shed and waited patiently for me to fasten the chain round her neck. Within ten minutes she was in a wild frenzy, tugging at her chain, bellowing frantically, soaked with sweat and shaking with fear. We knew of nothing that could have caused such alarm – but there was no doubt about it – she was quite simply terrified.

We could not leave her in the stall like that; we had to release her. She stumbled out into the yard, still bellowing and shaking and picking her feet up in a peculiar manner, as if the ground beneath were electrified. We managed to coax her into a loose box, well away from the cow shed, and eventually she lay down in a cowering heap.

I telephoned the vet. When he arrived, about an hour later, she was much quieter, though still trembling and coated in sweat. He examined her but could find nothing organically wrong. 'I don't know what the devil's the matter with her,' he said. 'It's obvious that she's been frightened almost to death. You'd think she'd been bewitched.'

Now, what he did not know, and for that matter, what I had forgotten until then, was an incident of that previous morning. There had been rain and the roadmen who had been working close by had come into my barn for shelter, as they had done on similar occasions. And as it was wet, I had stood in the barn talking to them. One of them, a comparative newcomer to the gang, a tall, gaunt man, with deepset far-away eyes, had said, apropos of nothing, that he could foretell the future, put spells on dogs and perform similar strange and occult deeds.

I was sceptical, indeed I scoffed at him. The other men remained silent, and at a much later date two of them told me it had been unwise to make light of their companion's powers, once he had foreseen a man's death in a ditch, and within a week his body had been found, not in, but close enough to a ditch to make people remember his words with apprehension. This strange roadman had obviously been put out by my doubts for he did not speak to me again. The sun came out, the man left, and I returned to my work and forgot about the incident ... until the vet's remark.

Humphrey Phelps
*Gloucestershire & Avon Life*, April 1978

# A Noise in the Pit

In the year 1840, or thereabouts, there was a man missing from the neighbourhood of Ruardean Hill, a stone-mason by trade, known by the nickname of 'Get-it-to-go.' He was last seen at a place where they sold drink; there was a report of a quarrel and some blows being struck, it was thought that the stone-cutter got what we Foresters call an unlucky blow – there was no police to find out the right thing. In a twelve-months' time it was rumoured that there was a noise heard in the old pit. There was a family living in the cabin close by the pit, and they said it seemed like a man boring a hole with a hammer and drill. The rumour spread and the parish constables were ordered to make a search. A windlass was put up and a search was made, but the body was not found, and the ghost was left to mind the pit for twelve or eighteen months longer. At length the noise in the pit or in the conscience of somebody, got worse and louder, and the constables were to have a horse wheel put up and a thorough search to be made. If my memory serve me right, they could not find him, but the noise increased and the bottom of the pit was cleaned up, and the stone-cutter's body was found, and his clothes helped to keep the body together to shovel it into the coffin. I saw the coffin landed and took out into the green for the people to see, which ought not to have been done. The wonder was that scores did not die from the horrid stench, it was reported that one person died from blood poison. There were from one hundred to a thousand people at the pit the day he was brought up.

Timothy Mountjoy
*The Life of a Forest of Dean Collier* (1887)

# Saved by a New Smock

How a waggoner from Newent way was saved from being smashed to pieces through having on a new frock, buttoned up to the chin. Forty-five years ago a great portion of the coal got in the Forest went into our nearest town. I have counted 35 waggons and carts going in the direction of Gloucester and Cheltenham, also a great number towards Hereford and Newent. A great many used to come to the pit before daylight. One of these men that came for coal, after putting the horses some food, went wandering about on the pit bank, and stepped right into the pit, close upon 100 yards deep; but the strength and depth of the frock acted like a balloon, and let him down in safety, so that he escaped without a finger being broken; no doubt the fright and the strange feeling that crept over him as he was falling he will never forget.

Timothy Mountjoy
*The Life of a Forest of Dean Collier* (1887)

# Cider-Drinking

Drinking a gallon-bottle-full at a draught is said to be no uncommon feat. A mere boyish trick, which will not bear to be bragged of. But to drain a two-gallon bottle without taking it from the lips, as a labourer of the vale is said to have done, by way of being even with master, who had paid him short in money – is spoken of as an exploit, which carried the art of draining a wooden bottle to its full pitch. Two gallons of cider, however, are not a stomach-full. Another man of the vale undertook, for a trifling wager, to drink twenty pints, one immediately after another. He got down nineteen (as the story is gravely told) but these filling the cask to the bung, the twentieth of course could not get admittance: so that a Severn-man's stomach holds exactly two gallons three pints.

William Marshall
*The Rural Economy of Gloucestershire*, Volume I, (1789)

# The Countryside in Wartime

# Arrival of Evacuees

All we knew then, and that mainly from hearsay, was that when an adult was billeted on you you got five shillings a week from the Post Office, and she was expected to buy her own food and cook it on your stove if you let her. It was made pretty clear that you were expected to let her do that, but no other details appeared to have been considered at all. Nothing about washing up, nothing about bedding, nothing about fuel, nothing about cooking utensils. It sounded like a fine source of trouble and quarrels all round to us, 'worse than the war', and we congratulated ourselves on the ninety children. Whatever a child does you can't very well quarrel with it, and in our experience in Auburn half the trouble in a lifetime comes from quarrels.

Meanwhile it was nearly three o'clock in the afternoon, very hot and very dusty. We began to worry they would not get down in time for them to have their tea and get safely installed before the black-out. Mrs Moore hoped they hadn't been travelling all day and wondered if they wouldn't be starving, and Doey said he'd been informed that they would all have rations.

Presently Mr Moore shouted from the playground, and we all popped out; but it was only a big covered van arriving. It swung down through the elm avenue and pulled up outside the school. The driver and his mate turned out of their seats like automatons, opened the doors, and began to drag out wooden food cases. They did not smile or speak or look at us. They brought the stuff straight in, dumped it in a corner and went back for more, moving quickly and as if they were working in their sleep. It was the first time war strain had come to Auburn, and it was odd and impressive, like the first pull of ack-ack fire in a blue sky. They looked as though they had been at work for seventy-two hours, as they probably had. There were red rims round their eyes, and their faces were grey and dirty. When someone asked them about the evacuees they snapped at us, and one man took off his coat, rolled it in a ball and threw it in a corner. Then he put his head on it and went to sleep.

Thinking it over, we were curiously unexcited by all this when one considers how interested we usually are when anything a little bit different arrives. We expected excitement, I suppose, and were saving it for the children. At any rate we took no notice of the sleeping man or his lorry, as far as I remember, apart from regarding them both stolidly. We examined the stores. There were quantities of it; bully beef, two sorts of tinned milk, and a considerable number of tins of biscuits as well as several quires of brown paper shopping bags.

Doey said suspiciously, 'There's a lot there, isn't there?' But at that moment a message came over from the Lion to say that eight buses were on their way. This delighted us all, and Mrs Moore got the kettles boiling. We were fidgeting about making last-minute preparations, when Doey, who had been thinking over the message, suddenly said, 'Eight buses?'

I said, 'Oh, they'll be those little old-fashioned charabancs things.' And he said, 'Very likely.'

I was wrong. Mrs Moore, who was by the big window which looks on to the road, saw them first. There they were, as foreign-looking as elephants. There were eight of them, big red double-decker London buses, the kind that carries thirty-two passengers on each floor, and as far as we could see they were crowded. They pulled up, a long line all down the road, with a London taxicab behind them. A small army of drivers and officials sprang out, shouting instructions to their passengers.

It was a difficult moment. We locals were all doing arithmetic. Twice thirty-two is sixty-four; eight times sixty-four is five hundred and twelve; and the entire population of Auburn is under six hundred and fifty. We hoped, we trusted, that there had been some mistake.

It was at this point that Doey made the second discovery. They weren't children. They were strange London-dressed ladies, all very tired and irritable, with babies in their arms.

We attempted to explain to the drivers, but all the time we were doing it it was slowly dawning upon us that we should never succeed. The drivers and the officials expected us to be hostile. They had read the newspapers. They were very tired, and moreover they were so nervy and exhausted, more with the emotional effort than anything else, that they were raw and spoiling for trouble. Doey and I, on the other hand, were just plain terrified. Finally, we persuaded them to wait for just ten minutes while we found out if there had been a mistake, and we all went into the Lion to telephone authority at Fishling.

Authority at Fishling sounded a bit rattled also, and we gathered that our difficulties were as nothing beside the troubles of others, and that we'd kindly get on with what God and the German Chancellor had seen fit to send us. So we said 'All right,' and went back. It was the beginning of the war for us in Auburn, the first real start of genuine trouble.

Fortunately there was plenty to do. As a reception committee we had hardly shone, and the immediate need seemed to be to remove any unfortunate first impressions.

To our intense relief the buses proved to be not quite full. There were just over three hundred souls altogether, many of them infants, but they looked like an army. They trooped into the school, spread over the rooms and the playground and sat down, all looking at us with tired, expectant eyes.

There appeared to be no one actually in charge of them now they had arrived. The bus drivers went away with the buses, and the two schoolmasters and one young schoolmistress who had come down with them were due to rush back as soon as possible to rejoin their own schools evacuated somewhere else in the east country.

The utter forlornness of the newcomers was quite theatrical. To our startled country eyes their inexpensive but very fashionable city clothes were grand if unsuitable, and with the myriads of babies in arms and the weeping toddlers hanging to their skirts they looked like everybody's long-lost erring daughter turned up to the old homes together in one vast paralysing emotional surprise.

Margery Allingham
*The Oaken Heart* (1941)

# Not Communicative

A few miles below Ross I inquired of three men in Home Guard uniform how I might best find my way to Goodrich. At first they were not communicative. They seemed, in fact, a little suspicious. But when I showed them my own Home Guard enrolment card, their manner changed. They were waiting for a bus which was to take them to their headquarters for a field-day. One of them was a farmer, another was an ex-jockey, the third had been a soldier.

'If I was to tell you the trouble I've 'ad this year with phlebitis in me legs and wireworms in me farm you wouldn't believe it. Shocking, I tell you. Never did see such wireworms, and as to me legs –'

'You wouldn't 'a' done in the Khyber Pass,' interrupted the soldier; ''ad to be fit out there to dodge the boulders the niggers rolled down on you.'

'One scratch on my legs and they don't heal for a six month,' continued the farmer.

'I wish they'd gove us 'orses,' said the jockey. 'I reckon a 'orse worth six cars across country.'

'Civvy 'orses no good under fire,' said the soldier, 'not trained to it.'

'We ain't got ter stand under fire,' replied the jockey. 'We got ter nip along and hinform.'

'I wonder how many of us could hit a parachutist?' I ventured.

'No 'arder than a peacock,' said the soldier. 'Ever shot peacocks, sir? Fine sport that. I shot twenty of 'em before breakfast in the jungle. They're fine eating all right too.'

Before I could hear further murderous details the khaki-laden coach appeared, and I was left to continue my way.

Robert Gibbings
*Coming Down the Wye* (1942)

# Landgirls

While the gang was working on the sugar beet Beryl and Elsie were weeding corn, in between milking times. Pat too helped when not engaged in horse-hoeing the potatoes, and the three landgirls had a pleasant time during the sunny weather. Then the weather broke, and they found weeding corn anything but pleasant. The water ran off the green corn into their boots. The corn was getting high, and the wet leaves soaked through breeches and gaiters till their clothes stuck cold and wet around knees and legs. They walked home at night with water oozing and sucking in their boots at each step.

One thing they had greatly missed since becoming landgirls, was the daily bath. The farmhouse boasted a bathroom, having been modernized since Jack Meadows succeeded his father as tenant of Heldon Wick. But the bath seemed to be the special possession of Mistress Meadows, probably it was fitted up at her suggestion, for it's no use glossing over the fact that the ordinary British farmer does not spend his mornings in the bath. Anyhow, the girls soon found out that though Mistress Meadows had given them a warm welcome to Heldon, it did not include very much warm water.

The chief reason for this lack was the fact that the water supply had to be pumped up out of a cistern under the scullery floor, to a tank somewhere on the house-top. Fifteen minutes each morning the maid spent at the pump handle, forcing sufficient water up to supply the ordinary everyday needs for domestic purposes. So if anyone used the bath – excepting the missus – it required another five minutes on the pump handle. The girls had willingly offered to spend five minutes every day pumping, but the mistress had no intention of pampering landgirls, and rather grudgingly allowed them the use of her bathroom on Saturday afternoons only.

Certainly it was an innovation for a farm worker to indulge in a bath. Farm lads washed their neck and ears and were considered as clean and decent as any other class of workers, and 'what is covered won't catch the dust,' is the general opinion. Perhaps the farmhouse sheets suffered for this opinion, but the rule was, if a farm lad wanted a more particular ablution, he got the wash-bowl from the scullery sink, and soaked his feet in it.

There he could sit soaking and smoking and wearing enough clothes to allow the most proper of mistresses or maids to pass through the scullery without feeling embarrassed.

The lack of a bathroom worried Pat more than it did her two companions. They were working in the dairy, and were not exposed to the dust and dirt as Pat was. Working in the fields during the dry weather her clothes had become full of dry sand. When the rain came and Pat was sent into the wet corn, the sand was washed through to her skin.

The girls sat one night in their bedroom. It had been a

wretched wet day, and coming home thoroughly soaked they had run up to their room to change before tea. They were all feeling rather glum as they peeled off their wet garments.

Pat ruefully surveyed her wet legs, striped in black and white markings. 'I never was so disgustingly filthy in my life. Come along, girls, let's go and ask Mrs Meadows for a bath.'

Very scantily attired, they swooped downstairs in search of the mistress.

Mrs Meadows looked up with surprise as three figures, dressed like dancing girls at a pantomime, came bursting in upon her. 'Good gracious!' she exclaimed.

'Please, Mrs Meadows,' began Pat, 'may we have a bath? Just look ... we're absolutely disgusting.'

'Disgusting?' echoed Mrs Meadows, 'I should think you are disgusting, coming downstairs like that. Go back and get dressed at once, girls, before Mr Meadows comes in!'

But at that moment Jack Meadows came stamping indoors. After a first gasp of surprise he grinned, and asked if they had started a nudist colony.

Pat explained the situation, showing her grimy legs, and after a brief discussion it was agreed that the girls should use the bathroom whenever the occasion demanded.

Having got over that difficulty the girls did not so much mind getting wet, and taking the wet with the fine, quite enjoyed weeding the corn until nearly hay-time.

Fred Kitchen
*The Farming Front* (1943)

# A Landgirl and Her Cheese

[Landgirls and other farmworkers but not farmers got an extra allowance of cheese during the war. This incident took place in 1942.]

Tilly was fond of her cheese and because of her calling she could get an extra supply. Mary, my wife, said: 'Tilly wants her cheese. Please ask Meg for her cards.'

Meg said: 'They aren't stamped yet; you didn't give me the money; shall I get stamps or will you?'

I said: 'Give me the cards; I will get the stamps.'

I queued up at the post-office. At last, when my turn came, the girl waved me away. She said: 'You must go to the other (auxiliary) office.'

So I queued up again and the new post-office girl said: 'You need to fill up a form and we have run out of these forms.'

So I said: 'What is this: the House that Jack built? My landgirl wants some cheese. She wants the cheese she gets with a coupon she gets with a card which needs a stamp which needs a form ...'

'Oh no,' said the girl. 'I thought it was clothing you were after. If it's only a stamp, you can get it in the other office.'

So I went back and queued again. Then when my turn came the girl said: 'Hullo, are you back again?'

I said: 'Yes. I'm still here, please can I have a 3d stamp for this card?'

'Higher up,' she said.

So I went and queued up again and when my turn came, the girl looked hard for a 3d stamp and said: 'Sorry, out of stock.'

So I went back to Meg and said: 'I can't get one; you have a try please.'

So Meg went out to some other post office I suppose and came back with a stamp which I stuck on the card which I carried back to Mary who gave it to Mollie who gave it back to Mary who said to me: 'Will you take it to the food office to get her cheese coupons with it, please?'

So I went to the food office and gave the girl Tilly's card and asked for the cheese coupons. The girl looked at the card and said: 'You have stuck this stamp in the wrong place.'

So I went back to Mary and told her and she said, 'Oh, well, you must get another stamp, I suppose.'

I said, 'What, me?'

She said, 'Yes.'

I said: 'No. Excuse me, dear. Give Tilly threepence and the card and tell her what to do.'

So Tilly got the coupons and gave them to Mary who took them to the shop to be registered and when this was all done and Mary thought she had nearly got Tilly's cheese, the shopman said: 'Sorry, no cheese to-day.'

Clifton Reynolds
*Glory Hill Farm (Second Year)* (1943)

# 'Get on to the Air Ministry'

These demonstrations and the strategy to force the Ford Motor Company of Britain to drop its trusty but unsophisticated old Fordson Tractor and put the Ferguson System tractor into production in its place were to culminate in a presentation of the tractor to the Ford Motor Company and British government officials in early May 1940. With the assistance of Trevor Knox, who it will be remembered had remained in Britain when most of the Ferguson team went to Detroit, a large demonstration was organised at St Stephens, Bedford. Lord Perry, the then Chairman of the Ford Motor Company, attended with many senior government officials.

During the final preparations for the demonstration, the quiet was continuously being disrupted by aircraft of the Royal Air Force passing overhead on their way to assist the embattled troops retreating towards Dunkirk. Ferguson was so irritated that he beckoned to a Ford public relations man who was in attendance.

'I can't give a demonstration with this noise going on,' he said, 'get on to the Air Ministry and ask them to reroute their aeroplanes away from here.'

The astonished Ford executive began to protest that such a thing could not be done, but he was cut short.

'Tell them it's a matter of national importance,' said Ferguson. 'It's just as important as fighting the war.'

The public relations man went away to do as bidden, but he met with no success.

Colin Fraser
*Harry Ferguson, Inventor and Pioneer* (1972)

# Poultry Rationing in Wartime

A very aggrieved poultry farmer reports a farcical state of affairs under the new poultry-food rationing scheme. After obeying the original Government suggestion that poultry-keepers should kill off most of their older laying birds, only to find the acutest shortage of eggs ever known as the result, she found herself with something over two hundred birds. For these she received twenty coupons. She was therefore a little astonished, when comparing notes with other poultry-keepers in the local market, to find not only that this ratio was nowhere consistent at all, but that one farmer, with twenty birds, had one thousand coupons. Country markets are excitable places, and it is just possible that a sense of grievance has inflated these figures a little. But, even allowing for that, this remains a strange manifestation of the official mind. But the postscript is stranger. To the protest of the poultry-keeper that poultry-keeping was becoming an impossible, if not farcical thing, the officials had a most comforting answer: 'We suggest,' they said, 'that you keep cows instead.'

H.E. Bates
*Country Life* (1943)

# Travel

# Well-Informed

We travelled with one of those troublesome fellow passengers in a stagecoach, that is called a well-informed man. For twenty miles we discoursed about the properties of steam, probabilities of carriage by ditto, till all my science, and more than all, was exhausted, and I was thinking of escaping my torment by getting up on the outside when, getting into Bishop's Stortford, my gentleman, spying some farming land, put an unlucky question to me: 'What sort of crop of turnips do you think we shall have this year?' Emma's eyes turned to me, to know what in the world I could have to say; and she burst into a violent fit of laughter, maugre her pale, serious cheeks, when, with the greatest gravity, I replied: 'It depends, I believe, upon boiled legs of mutton.' ... I am afraid my credit sank very low with my fellow traveller, who had thought he had met with a well-informed passenger, which is an accident so desirable in a stage-coach.

Charles Lamb, 1810

# Miles Out of His Way

'Either,' said I, 'you did not know the way well, or you did; if the former, it was dishonest in you to undertake to guide me; if the latter, you have wilfully led me miles out of my way.' He grumbled, but off he went. He certainly deserved nothing; for he did not know the way, and he prevented some other man from earning and receiving the money. But, had he not caused me to get upon Hindhead, he would have had the three shillings. I had, at one time, got my hand in my pocket, but the thought of having been beaten pulled it out again.

William Cobbett, 24 November 1822
*Rural Rides*

# Travelling 'Outside'

The ride from Leicester to Northampton I shall remember as long as I live.

The coach drove from the yard through a part of the house. The inside passengers got in, in the yard; but we on the outside were obliged to clamber up in the public street, because we should have had no room for our heads to pass under the gateway.

My companions on the top of the coach were a farmer, a young man very decently dressed, and a blackamoor.

The getting up alone was at the risk of one's life; and when I was up, I was obliged to sit just at the corner of the coach, with nothing to hold by, but a sort of little handle, fastened on the side. I sat nearest the wheel; and the moment that we set off, I fancied that I saw a certain death await me. All I could do was to take still faster hold of the handle, and to be more and more careful to preserve my balance.

The machine now rolled along with prodigious rapidity, over the stones through the town, and every moment we seemed to fly into the air; so that it was almost a miracle that we still stuck to the coach and did not fall. We seemed to be thus on the wing and to fly, as often as we passed through a village, or went down a hill.

At last the being continually in fear of my life became insupportable, and as we were going up a hill, and consequently proceeding rather slower than usual, I crept from the top of the coach and got snug into the basket.

'O, sir, sir, you will be shaken to death!' said the black; but I flattered myself that he exaggerated the unpleasantness of my post.

As long as we went up hill, it was easy and pleasant. And, having had little or no sleep the night before, I was almost asleep among the trunks and the packages; but how was the case altered when we came to go downhill; then all the trunks and parcels began, as it were, to dance around me, and everything in the basket seemed to be alive; and I every moment received from them such violent blows that I thought my last hour was come. I now found that what the black had told me was no exaggeration; but all my complaints were useless. I was obliged to suffer this torture nearly an hour, till we came to another hill again, when, quite shaken to pieces and sadly bruised, I again crept to the top of the coach and took possession of my former seat. 'Ah, did I not tell you that you would be shaken to death?' said the black as I was getting up; but I made no reply. Indeed I was ashamed; and I now write this as a warning to all strangers to stage-coaches who may happen to take it into their heads, without being used to it, to take a place on the outside of an English post-coach; and still more, a place in the basket.

About midnight we arrived at Harborough, where I could only rest myself a moment, before we were again called to set off, full drive, through a number of villages, so that a few hours before daybreak we had reached Northampton, which is, however, thirty-three miles from Leicester.

From Harborough to Northampton I had a most dreadful journey, it rained incessantly, and as before we had been covered with dust, we now were soaked with rain. My neighbour, the young man who had sat next me in the middle, that my inconveniences might be complete, every now and then fell asleep; and as, when asleep, he perpetually bolted and rolled against me, with the whole weight of his body, more than once he was very near pushing me entirely off my seat.

We at last reached Northampton, where I immediately went to bed, and have slept almost till noon. Tomorrow morning I intend to continue my journey to London in some other stage coach.

Carl Philipp Moritz
*Travels Through Several Parts of England in 1782*

# The Stile

One day I stopped by the stile at the corner to say good-bye to a friend who had walked thus far with me. It was about half an hour after the sunset of a dry, hot day among the many wet ones in that July. We had been talking easily and warmly together, in such a way that there was no knowing whose was any one thought, because we were in electrical contact and each leapt to complete the other's words, just as if some poet had chosen to

use the form of an eclogue and had made us the two shepherds
who were to utter his mind through our dialogue. When he
spoke I had already the same thing in the same words to express.
When either of us spoke we were saying what we could not have
said to any other man at any other time.

But as we reached the stile our tongues and our steps ceased
together, and I was instantly aware of the silence through which
our walking and talking had drawn a thin line up to this point.
We had been going on without looking at one another in the
twilight. Now we were face to face. We wished to go on speaking
but we could not. My eyes wandered to the rippled outline of the
dark heavy hills against the sky, which was now pale and barred
with the grey ribs of a delicate sunset. High up I saw Gemma, I
even began trying to make out the bent star bow of which it is
the centre. I saw the plain, now a vague dark sea of trees and
hedges, where lay my homeward path. Again I looked at the face
near me, and one of us said:

'The weather looks a little more settled.'

The other replied: 'I think it does.'

I bent my head and tapped the toe of my shoe with my stick,
wishing to speak, wishing to go, but aware of a strong unknown
power which made speech impossible and yet was not violent
enough to detach me altogether and at once from the man
standing there. Again my gaze wandered dallying to the hills – to
the sky and the increase of stars – the darkness of the next hedge
– the rushy green, the pale roads and the faint thicket mist that
was starred with glow-worms. The scent of the honeysuckles
and all those hedges was in the moist air. Now and then a few
unexpected, startled, and startling words were spoken, and the
silence drank them up as the sea drinks a few tears. But always
my roving eyes returned from the sky, the hills, the plain to those
other greenish eyes in the dusk, and then with a growing sense
of rest and love to the copse waiting there, its definite cloud of
leaves and branches and, above that, the outline of oak-tops
against the sky. It was very near. It was still, sombre, silent. It
was vague and unfamiliar, I had forgotten that it was a copse and
one that I had often seen before. White roses like moths
penetrated the mass of the hedge.

I found myself saying 'Goodbye'. I heard the word 'goodbye'
spoken. It was a signal not of a parting but of a uniting. In spite
of the unwillingness to be silent with my friend a moment

before, a deep ease and confidence was mine beneath that unrest. I took one or two steps to the stile.

Edward Thomas
*Light and Twilight* (Duckworth, 1911)

# The Footpath

There was a place on my one-inch ordnance map, about halfway between Arford and the Beacon Hill at Hindhead, which was called the Land of Nod. Nobody whom I asked was able to tell me what sort of a place it might be, nor why it was called the Land of Nod, so after luncheon I set off, feeling rather whimsical and De La Mareish, to discover and explore it.

The way led past the edge of Wishanger Common and along narrow by-roads to a hamlet called Barford; but my map showed a footpath off the Churt road which was quite as direct and would certainly be pleasanter to walk on. Accordingly I turned left at the second crossroads, and reaching the point where the footpath apparently started, I walked boldly into a farmyard and tried to open the gate into a field. It was uncomprisingly tied up with chains and padlocks, and while I was fiddling with it, a very angry woman bustled out of the farmhouse and asked me sharply what I wanted. I explained that I wanted the footpath to Barford.

'Oh, you can go along the road to Barford,' she said.

'I know, but I want to go along the path.'

'There isn't a path,' she said firmly.

'There's one on my map.'

'Then your map's wrong. This is our place.'

She was so stern and determined that I thought I had perhaps made a mistake after all; I apologised for my intrusion, and went back on to the road. From about fifty yards farther on, however, I could see quite clearly the track running across the field behind the farmhouse, the stile into the next field, and the path winding on beyond. Out of sheer obstinacy I climbed over the fence and made towards the track. As I did so three small children in bathing dresses, who were sitting in the shallow stream that ran along the bottom of the field, got up and waved at me.

'Oy,' they said, 'you can't go there. It's our place.'

The children splashed about in agitation.

'You can't,' they shouted. 'No footpath. Our place.'

'Oh, shut up about your place,' I said.

The cries of these extremely possessive children followed me as I went up the hill.

'Our place, our place, our place!'

Long before I reached the footpath the old woman was out again. She shouted after me:

'I've told you can't get to Barford that way.'

'Can't I?' I said. 'I'll bet you.'

'If you break any fences –' she warned.

I hurried on till I could no longer hear what she was shouting. I joined the footpath, which was wide, well-marked and apparently public; the field through which it ran was dotted with the little mushroom-like tents of hikers. In the next field, however, it became the merest sheep-track; and in the third field it petered out altogether, and I found myself walking through a patch of uncut clover in which there was no semblance of a track at all. I was not a bit surprised when the farmer himself, an old prophetic man with a beard, bore down upon me fiercely and shouted: 'Hey, you can't –'

I had the answer by now.

'It's your place, isn't it?' I said, smiling sweetly.

The magic formula worked.

'Well, it is that,' he said. 'And there's no footpath.'

'I'm sorry. The ordnance map shows one. Have a look.'

At this he fell into a great rage.

'That so-and-so map,' he said.

'Why,' I asked, 'have you had trouble like this before?'

'Trouble!' he shouted. 'I should think I have had trouble. And they all show me the map. The so-and-so map's wrong, I tell you. There's no right of way; and if there was a path once, it's ploughed up by now, and fenced up, and nobody can get along it without breaking the fences down. It's all the fault of the so-and-so Government. They shouldn't put a footpath on the map if there isn't one.'

I explained gently:

'You see, the footpath's marked on the map because there was a footpath when the map was surveyed. But that doesn't prove it's a right of way. It may be just a private footpath across –' I smiled again – 'across your place.'

'Is that true?' he said excitedly. 'Can I tell that to the so-and-so hikers when they show me the map?'

'Yes. You can say that the fact the footpath's shown on the map isn't evidence that they've the right to go along it. But of course if there is a right of way they could take you to court about it.'

'I'll take them to court, the so-and-sos.'

'Then you can fight it out and get it settled.'

''Tis a fair puzzle,' said the old man.

'It's a fair puzzle how I'm going to get out of this field,' I said. He grinned.

'You can get over the fence by the corner.'

'You don't mind?'

'Not you. But when those so-and-so hikers wave that map in my face, and stand here on my place argyfying that they've got a right to be on it, that gets my goat, it does. You go on, and good luck to you.'

I needed his good wishes. The fence was well nigh impenetrable. I scratched myself all over climbing it. The next field was huge and empty. I toiled across it under a blazing sun, and I had just taken off my shirt for coolness' sake when I heard an angry voice roaring at me from behind the hedge:

'Now you come out of that bloody field quick.'

By this time I was beginning to feel as a hunted fox must feel. In some curious way my lack of a shirt to my back seemed to place me at a disadvantage. The owner of the angry voice apparently thought so too, for he now appeared from behind the hedge and yelled at me:

'I'll have the law on you. Walking half naked and as bold as brass through my fields. I'll have you up for trespass.'

'Tripe,' I said: but with less conviction that I should have had if I had been properly shirted.

'Tripe, indeed! You say Tripe, do you? You dare to stand there and say Tripe!'

'You see you can't have me up,' I said wearily. 'You're talking through your hat. You can't have me up for trespass. I haven't broken any law. In any case the farmer over there said I could come this way –'

'This isn't his field.'

'Oh well, I'm sorry.'

'You get out of it bloody quick.'

I did. And at last I reached Barford, but not before I had been abused and threatened with the law by two more people – a farm labourer, and a man in breeches who looked like a groom or second-horseman. For almost the first time in my life I was glad to be walking on a hard highroad again. I hastened as swiftly as I might out of the ill-mannered and litigious parish of Barford.

John Moore
*A Walk Through Surrey* (1939)

# On Such a Night

A much respected farmer was before the Bench on a charge of driving at night without lights. 'I'm sorry to see a man like you brought up before me,' said the magistrate. 'Well,' said the farmer, ''twould have been an insult to God Almighty to have had a light on a night like that.'

H.J. Massingham
*A Countryman's Journal* (1939)

# Forest Humour

Having finished my business at a small and very remote farm I enquired where I should find Mr M., who, according to my list, lived at a smaller and even more remote farm. I was given detailed instructions, including reference to several trees of various shapes, and a careful description of the dog at the cottage where Mr M., did not live. I moved on, expressing thanks as I went, when my guide called out, 'Thee'll have to hurry, mind.' I asked if Mr M., was known to be going out, to which the reply came, 'Ay, they'm putting 'e under in 'arf-hour, see.'

F.W. Baty
*The Forest of Dean* (1952)

# The Elements

# 25 May 1776

The frost has killed the tops of the walnut shoots, and ashes; and the annuals where they touched the glass of the frames; also many kidney beans. The tops of hops and potatoes were cut-off by this frost. Tops of laurels killed. The walnut-trees promised for a vast crop, 'til the shoots were cut off by ye frost. No one that has not attended to such matters, and taken down remarks, can be aware how much ten days dripping weather will influence the growth of grass or corn after a severe dry season. This present summer 1776 yields a remarkable instance: for 'til the 30th of May the fields were burnt-up and naked, and the barley not half out of the ground; but now, June 10th there is an agreeable prospect of plenty. A very intelligent Clergyman assured me, that hearing while he was a young student at the University, of toads being found alive in blocks of stone, and solid bodies of trees; he one long vacation took a toad, and put it into a garden-pot, and laying a tile over the mouth of the pot, buried it five feet deep in the ground in his father's garden. In about 13 months he dug-up the imprisoned reptile, and found it alive and well, and considerably grown. He buried it again as at first, and on a second visit at about the same period of time found it circumstanced as before. He then deposited the pot as formerly a third time, only laying the tile so as not quite to cover the whole of its mouth: But when he came to examine it again next year, the toad was gone. He each time trod the earth down very hard over the pot.

Gilbert White
*Journals*

## Winter

January 15th, 1794; The Weather most piercing, severe frost, with Wind and some Snow, the Wind from the East and very rough. Last night was the severest we have yet had. It froze so sharp within doors that the milk in the Milk-pans in the Dairy was froze in a Mass.

January 23rd: The weather more severe than ever, it froze apples within doors tho' covered with a thick carpet.

January 25th: The frost this morning more severe than yesterday. It froze last Night the Chamber Pots above Stairs.

January 28th: Very severe frost indeed, freezes sharp within doors and bitter cold it is now. Two Women froze to death Saturday last going from Norwich Market to their home ... I was saying before dinner that there would be an alteration of Weather as soon as I a long time observed one of our Cats wash over both her Ears – an old observation and now I must believe it to be a pretty true one.

James Woodforde
*The Diary of a Country Parson*

# Tribulations

We had got all our hay in the very best manner, and the crops of corn seemed smiling in every field around us, whilst the continuation of unusually warm summer weather filled every heart with joy. On the day of the disaster I had a picnic party here of about one hundred and twenty people. After passing a delightful afternoon in singing and in dancing, there seemed to be no reason why their festivities should not be continued till the edge of dark; but, about half past seven, distant peals of grumbling thunder forewarned us that mischief was on the stir. The people ordered the three omnibuses, etc., in which they had come, to get ready for departure; but I desired them not to think of going away. The storm which was slowly approaching, might catch them on their journey and, as there were as many outside as inside passengers, they would not fail to get steeped with rain; and my advice to them was, 'Stay where you are: there is abundant shelter close at hand.' They followed my advice. Some got into the vehicles in the stable-yard, while others took shelter in the temples at the pleasure grounds. Down came the rain in torrents, equal to anything I had ever seen in the tropics.

The thunder roared incessantly, and the lightning flashed with fearful brilliancy, whilst the clouds assumed a red and yellow colour, which I had never observed before. We were all of us in the house, and astounded at what was going on in the heavens above us. Suddenly there fell, in countless numbers, hailstones – some as large as pullet-eggs. They broke eighty-one large glass squares in the front of the house, and drove the fragments of glass from the windows to the opposite wall in the room where we were standing. One flash of lightning seemed to be in the very midst of us. It struck a cherry tree close to the stables. A woman in one of the carriages was holding her parasol outside of the window, in order to prevent the rain from entering. The parasol was struck and broken by the lightning, whilst her forefinger, and arm up to the elbow, was rendered perfectly numb, without having received the slightest wound. Nearly all the panes of glass in the hot-house were smashed to atoms. This was about all the injury we received at Walton Hall. My garden and corn-fields, potatoes and turnips, were spared. Not so in the village and the neighbourhood. Whole fields of wheat, barley, oats, turnips, and potatoes have been entirely destroyed. The ears of corn were cut from the stalks, and lay on the ground, as completely thrashed as though they had been under the flail. Acres of beans are now lying in absolute ruin, while entire gardens have to deplore the loss of their entire produce. I have almost forgot to mention that one man in the stable-yard was felled to the ground by a single hailstone. This I had from his own mouth.

Charles Waterton
*Essays on Natural History (1838-57)*

## A Very Great Storm

August 9th 1843. Long to be remembered. One of the most terrific hail-storms ever known in England. The first part of the morning was fine, and very close and hot. Heavy thunder in the distance. About 12 o'clock the storm drew nearer from the west and kept up one continued roar of thunder for an hour and a half without intermission, attended by vivid lightning. At a quarter past one the rain began falling in torrents, attended by a complete hurricane. It then began hailing (large pieces of ice falling) so fast and hard that our crops of corn during the half hour it lasted were all nearly destroyed; all the fruit was stripped from the trees and all the windows facing the storm were smashed in; the turnips were washed away or beaten into the land; cabbages have the appearance of having been knocked to pieces with sticks, and young vetches were cut up like salading. Father's wheat was nearly ripe but almost all so much thrashed out and the straw so completely shivered and knocked down that he had it all mown directly and carried it loose. Gave half-a-crown for mowing it per acre. The barley was just got well out into ear and even that did not escape a partial thrashing, although so green. What ears are left cannot ripen: the straw is so broken that the moisture cannot reach them. We are now mowing it in a green state for fodder. The oats are about three parts knocked out although quite green, and we are cutting them for fodder. We had some early peas cut and almost fit to carry and the hail beat all the peas on the overside out as fairly as if they had been thrashed. The beans are very much cut about. Some of the stalks as thick as my thumb are cut in two in several places; many of the pods are cut off and the beans in what are left are decaying from the bruises. We have had all the late peas hacked in a green state. The late-sown wheat that is in a green state is perfectly useless excepting as fodder.

I picked up several pieces of ice in the front garden, just after the storm, measuring from six to eight inches round, and weighed six averaging above an ounce each. There were much larger pieces picked up in the neighbourhood, measuring ten inches and upwards. Some of the ice did not melt for a fortnight. We had about a hundred panes of glass broken. Grandma had 300 broken in the front of her house at Little Tew. At Chipping Norton it is said £3000 will not put the glass in repair. Captain Cox at Sandford has about £200 of glass broken. Mr Radford's windows were smashed in, leads and all, and a cartload of slates knocked off the roof. Some of the pieces of ice cut through some new blue slates into Mr Coldicott's field barn at Sandford. A large flood from the storm washed a great deal of soil off the land. Some of the furrows are washed plough deep for a yard wide.

Several hares, rabbits, pheasants, partridges, pigeons, rooks, etc., have been picked up dead and little birds of all description out of number. One of Mr Grayham's men picked up seven dead rabbits in a piece of peas, and one of my father's men found eight dead rooks as he was going to Enstone. The young clover that we were mowing for the horses had nothing left but the bare stalks. The storm passed over Kingham, Salford, Chipping Norton, Tew, Sandford, Leadwell, the Wortons and passed on to Aston, etc. The road to the limekiln on Beaconsfield Farm was blocked up with ice from three to five feet deep. Mr Grayham was dipping lambs there and the flood swilled a pen of forty lambs, hurdles and dipping apparatus for some considerable distance. One of the hailstones hit a little boy (who was driving a plow for father at Little Tew) on his head and knocked him down. Mr Coldicott was carrying sainfoin seed at Sandford and an old bald-headed man was leading; hailstones cut his hat off and before he could get it again peppered his poor head so that the blood ran down his face. In Enstone field scarcely a hare escaped the storm, several brace being found dead in one piece of clover. The electric fluid killed two men near Clanvale and two horses at Broadwell.

'Diary of a Farmer of Great Tew, Oxfordshire'
*The Countryman* (Summer, 1945)

# Heavy Wind

But, of course, you wouldn't recollect the heavy wind. That's about seventy-five years ago. Well, that was a lovely Saturday. On the Sunday morning that started – the wind started blowing. And that was a funny, funny wind that was! That blow scores of trees down; cattle, horses on the meadow, some on 'em. It just took 'em up like that, and took 'em across: some were lying in the ditch, some in the hedge. And I've been wanting to ask if they got a record o' that at Pulham St Mary. The parson there, the chapel parson, he went there; and it just lifted the roof off the chapel like that and killed him in the pulpit, blew in the wall. As dead as a doornail ...

It took all the stacks up – tons and tons – and simply took 'em up like that off the ground and scattered them over the fields, I

know a man, Mr Pymar, Spencer Pymar who lives at Diss. His
father sent him after an owd man somewhere to come hoom;
and he had an owd pony. And the wind took him up pony and
all, and plumped him up against the hedge. He was telling me
about that not long ago.

To come back to the thrashing; I can recollect one little
incident. We were working on a farm, and I had a little dawg;
and another chap with me had a little dawg. And I think, if I
remember right, they killed around about 170 rats while we
were thrashing; and they had no netting round the stacks then.
Anyhow we finished; and when we were gathering the things
together, these little dogs they got a rabbit. And the farmer came
arter us in what you'd call a hurry. He would have prosecuted us
if it hadn't been for Mr Stevens – just because the dawgs go that
rabbit! He would have prosecuted us. Yeh! And he told Mr
Edgar Stevens:

'Never bring them men on my place no more!'

*Spoken History* (1987)
told to George Ewart Evans

# Clouds

I must here relate something that appears very interesting to me,
and something which, though it must have been seen by every
man that has lived in the country, or, at least, in any hilly
country, has never been particularly mentioned by anybody as
far as I can recollect. We frequently talk of clouds coming from
dews, and we actually see the heavy fogs become clouds. We see
them go up to the tops of the hills, and, taking a swim round,
come and drop down upon us and wet us through. But I am now
going to speak of clouds, coming out of sides of hills in exactly
the same manner that you see smoke come out of a
tobacco-pipe, and, rising up with a wider and wider head, like
the smoke from a tobacco-pipe, go to the top of the hill, or over
the hill, or very much above it, and then come down the valleys
in rain. At about a mile's distance from Mr Palmer's house at
Bollitree, in Herefordshire, there is a large, long, beautiful
wood, covering the side of a lofty hill, winding round in the form

of a crescent, the bend of the crescent being towards Mr Palmer's house. We stood and observed cloud after cloud come out from different parts of the side of the hill, and tower up and go over the hill out of sight. He told me that that was a certain sign that it would rain that day, for that these clouds would come back again and fall in rain. It rained sure enough; and I found that the country people all round about had this mode of the forming of the clouds as a sign of rain. The hill is called Penyard, and this forming of the clouds they call Old Penyard's smoking his pipe; and it is a rule that it is sure to rain during the day, if Old Penyard smokes his pipe in the morning. These appearances take place especially in warm and sultry weather. It was very warm yesterday morning: it had thundered violently the evening before; we felt it hot even when the rain fell upon us at Butser Hill. Petersfield lies in a pretty broad and very beautiful valley. On three sides of it are very lofty hills, partly downs and partly covered with trees; and, as we proceeded on our way from the bottom of Butser Hill to Petersfield, we saw thousands upon thousands of clouds continually coming puffing out from different parts of these hills and towering up to the top of them. I stopped George several times to make him look at them; to see them puffing out of the chalk downs as well as out of the woodland hills; and bade him remember to tell his father of it when he should get home, to convince him that the hills of Hampshire could smoke their pipes, as well as those of Herefordshire. This is a really curious matter. I have never read in any book anything to lead me to suppose that the observation has ever found its way into print before. Sometimes you will see only one or two clouds during a whole morning come out of the sides of a hill; but we saw thousands upon thousands bursting out, one after another, in all parts of these immense hills. The first time that I have leisure, when I am in the high countries again, I will have a conversation with some old shepherd about this matter; if he cannot enlighten me upon the subject, I am sure that no philosopher can.

William Cobbett, 23 October 1826
*Rural Rides*

# Cobwebs

On September the 21st, 1741, being then on a visit, and intent on field diversions, I rose before daybreak; when I came into the enclosures, I found the stubble and clover grounds matted all over with a thick coat of cobwebs, in the meshes of which a copious and heavy dew hung so plentifully, that the whole face of the country seemed, as it were, covered with two or three setting-nets, drawn one over another. When the dogs attempted to hunt, their eyes were so blinded and hoodwinked that they could not proceed, but were obliged to lie down and scrape the encumbrances from their faces with their forefeet; so that, finding my sport interrupted, I returned home, musing in my mind on the oddness of the occurrence.

As the morning advanced, the sun became bright and warm, and the day turned out one of those most lovely ones which no season but the autumn produces – cloudless, calm, serene, and worthy of the south of France itself.

About nine an appearance very unusual began to demand our attention, – a shower of cobwebs falling from very elevated regions, and continuing, without any interruption, till the close of the day.

These webs are not single filmy threads, floating in the air in all directions, but perfect flakes of rags; some near an inch broad, and five or six long, which fell with a degree of velocity which showed they were considerably heavier than the atmosphere.

On every side, as the observer turned his eyes, he might behold a continual succession of fresh flakes falling into his sight, and twinkling like stars, as they turned their sides towards the sun.

Gilbert White
*Natural History of Selbourne* (1789)

# Fall of Cliff

The months of January and February, in the year 1774, were remarkable for great melting snows and vast gluts of rain; so that by the end of the latter month, the land-springs, or levants, began to prevail, and to be near as high as in the memorable winter of 1764. The beginning of March also went on in the same tenor, when, in the night between the 8th and 9th of that month, a considerable part of the great woody hanger at Hawkley was torn from its place, and fell down, leaving a high free-stone cliff naked and bare, and resembling the steep side of a chalk pit. It appears that this huge fragment, being, perhaps, sapped and undermined by waters, foundered, and was ingulfed, going down in a perpendicular direction; for a gate, which stood in the field on the top of the hill, after sinking with its posts for thirty or forty feet, remained in so true and upright a position, as to open and shut with great exactness, just as in the first situation. Several oaks also are still standing, and in a state of vegetation, after taking the same desperate leap. The great part of this prodigious mass was absorbed in some gulf below, is plain also, from the inclining ground at the bottom of the hill, which is free and unencumbered, but would have been buried in heaps of rubbish, had the fragment parted and fallen forward. About a hundred yards from the foot of the hanging coppice, stood a cottage by the side of a lane; and two hundred yards lower, on the other side of the lane, was a farm-house, in which lived a labourer and his family; and just by, a stout new barn. The cottage was inhabited by an old woman and her son, and his wife. These people, in the evening, which was very dark and tempestuous, observed that the brick floors of their kitchens began to heave and part, and that the walls seemed to open, and the roofs to crack; but they all agree that no tremor of the ground, indicating an earthquake, was ever felt, only that the wind continued to make a most tremendous roaring in the woods and hangers. The miserable inhabitants, not daring to go to bed, remained in the utmost solicitude and confusion, expecting every moment to be buried under the ruins of their shattered edifices. When daylight came, they were at leisure to contemplate the devastations of the night. They then found that a deep rift, or chasm, had opened under their houses, and torn them, as it were, in two, and that one end of the barn had suffered in a similar manner: that a pond near the cottage had undergone a strange reverse, becoming deep at the shallow end, and so vice versa: that many large oaks were removed out of their perpendicular, some thrown down, and some fallen into the heads of neighbouring trees; and that a gate was thrust forward, with its hedge, full six feet, so as to require a new track to be made to it. From the foot of the cliff, the general course of the ground, which is pasture, inclines in a moderate descent for half a mile, and is interspersed with some hillocks, which were rifted in every direction, as well towards the great woody hanger as from it. In the first pasture the deep clefts began, and, running across the lane and under the buildings, made such vast shelves that the road was impassable for some time; and so over to an arable field on the other side, which was strangely torn and disordered. The second pasture field being more soft and springy, was protruded forward without many fissures in the turf, which was raised in long ridges resembling graves, lying at right angles to the motion. At the bottom of the enclosure, the soil and turf rose many feet against the bodies of some oaks that obstructed their further course, and terminated this awful commotion.

The perpendicular height of the precipice, in general, is twenty-three yards; the length of the lapse or slip, as seen from the fields below, one hundred and eighty-one: and a partial fall, concealed in the coppice, extends seventy yards more; so that the total length of this fragment that fell was two hundred and fifty-one yards. About fifty acres of land suffered from this violent convulsion; two houses were entirely destroyed; one end of a new barn was left in ruins, the walls being cracked through the very stones that composed them; a hanging coppice was changed to a naked rock; and some grass grounds and an arable field so broken and rifted by the chasms, as to be rendered, for a time, neither fit for the plough, nor safe for pasturage, till considerable labour and expense had been bestowed in levelling the surface, and filling in the gaping fissures.

Gilbert White
*Natural History of Selbourne* (1789)

# The Ways of God

'If,' she said once, 'if God's a Christian man, I do not know what he means by this weather.'

'I reckon he manages about as well as could be expected in

such a funny world,' replied her husband. 'Remember old Farmer King who used to swear at the weather so. One day when he had got his hay dry at last and saw it coming on to rain, he picks up a handful and stuffs it into his pocket, and says he will carry that much home dry at any rate, but if he didn't fall into the brook on his way back and get wet to the skin. Such are the ways of God.'

Edward Thomas
*The Heart of England* (Dent, 1906)

# A Country Miscellany

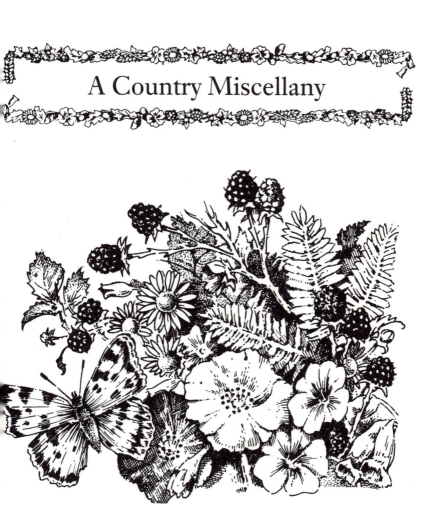

# Election of Parish Councillors

[Until 1949 the election of parish councillors was by a show of hands.]

The three-yearly election of Parish Councillors, a performance always accompanied by a certain hilarity, took place to-day. The supposedly, but not actually, representative gathering, perhaps one hundred and fifty in all for a thousand people, were divided into two halves. Four tellers, two for each side, were appointed to count the votes, recorded by show of hands. After the somewhat unaccountable fifteen minutes' legal pause, we began. When a quarter down the list of sixteen candidates (for eleven seats) it was discovered that, owing to a misunderstanding, one teller was counting all instead of half his company. With groans we began again from the beginning. This time the tellers for one side, completely disorganised, ceased to be able to count at all, and on three re-counts the votes of one candidate failed each time to tally! The chairman showed signs of despair, and the now desperate tellers declared that half the voters only waggled their hands instead of putting an arm up, so they could not see them. Chairman with a stroke of genius suggested that all voters for candidate should stand up. Enthusiastic supporters leapt to their feet, but it was shortly realised that half the meeting at the back was standing anyhow, and this was followed by cries of 'Not legal! Votes by show of hands only!'

The Chairman tore his remaining hairs in complete distraction, while almost hysterical tellers muttered numbers feverishly, their eyes rolling over a vastly amused company. Then the Chairman had the bright thought of changing over one teller from each side, and thus steadied all was well. At last, after an hour and a half, we emerged either crowned with laurels or draped in sackcloth and ashes, according to whether we had been elected or not.

Lilias Rider Haggard
*Norfolk Life* (1943)

# A Faux Pas

As Chairman of the Gloucestershire Federation of Women's Institutes, I attended a meeting of a local branch. I entered the hall and took a seat and one member came and sat by me and asked if I was a new member. I told her I was not a new member, so she then asked if I was a visitor and rather than explain who I was, I simply said 'Yes'.

'Oh, what a pity you've come tonight,' she replied, 'the County Chairman is our speaker tonight, and she's sure to be boring.'

Jill Warwick

# See the Man

I had not the Register by me, and could not detect the garbling. All the words that I have put in italics, this Hitchins left out in the reading. What sort of man he must be the public will easily judge – No sooner had Hitchins done, than up started Mr Ingram, a farmer of Rottendean, who was the second person in the drama (for all had been duly prepared), and moved that I should be put out of the room! Some few of the Webb Hallites joined by about six or eight of the dark, dirty-faced, half-whiskered, tax eaters from Brighton (which is only eight miles off) joined in this cry. I rose, that they might see the man that they had to put out. Fortunately for themselves, not one of them attempted to approach me. They were like the mice that resolved that a bell should be put round the cat's neck! – However, a considerable hubbub took place. At last, however, the Chairman, Mr Kemp, whose conduct was fair and manly, having given my health, I proceeded to address the company in substance as stated here below; and it is curious enough, that even those who, upon my health being given, had taken their hats and gone out of the room (and amongst whom Mr Ellman the younger was one) came back, formed a crowd, and were just as silent and attentive as the rest of the company!

William Cobbett
*Rural Rides*

# Insurance

In insurance against fire a higher rate is charged on thatch than on the other kinds of roofing; and I presume the higher rate is needed, though possibly for other reasons than the nature of the roof. Writing to my father about a small estate that was for sale, my grandfather remarks quite placidly, 13 June 1864: – 'The premises are all but new, for ***** took care to burn down the whole at different times – so all new and well built and slated. No office would continue the insurance for him, but being all slated it did not much require it.' I have heard the same thing said of other small estates.

There were many fires in Moreton about seventy or eighty years ago. In those times the insurance companies had fire engines of their own, and people trusted to these engines. After a fire there 11 September 1838, my father writes in his diary: – 'The Moreton engine poured on the thatch in front of Mrs Heyward's house, and kept the fire in the back premises. But, as the fire was extending towards the White Hart, which was insured in the "West of England," the engine (which belonged to that office) was removed there to endeavour to preserve the inn. As soon as the engine was removed, the fire came into the front of Mrs Heyward's house, and extended on in Pound Street … There ought to be two engines in the place; and, as the "Sun" lost so much, perhaps they will send one there.'

Cecil Torr
*Small Talk at Wreyland* (1979)

# Wedded and Buried

I remember a curious incident connected with the tap-root of an oak. This oak, a good tree of perhaps two hundred years' growth, was being felled in Bradenham Wood, in this county, when the woodman called attention to something peculiar on the tap-root. On clearing it of soil, we found that the object was a horse-shoe of ancient make. Obviously in the beginning an acorn must have fallen into the hollow of this cast shoe, and as it grew through the slow generations the root filled up the circle, carrying it down into the earth in the process of its increase, till at length we found wood and iron thus strangely wedded.

H. Rider Haggard
*A Farmer's Year* (Longmans, 1899)

# Doctor Knows Best

An old country tale came my way the other day which to my mind is of Wordsworthian quality: 'There might be some unkid (here, dreary) parsons about and farmers be a gallus (cunning and self-interested) lot mostly, but doctors be proper men. Folks about here respecks and trusts 'em, and rightly so it be. Poor old Daniel was mortal bad; and there lay he, white as a cloud and calm and still as a pool in summer time. 'Dear old chap! I'm afraid he's gone,' said the doctor. 'No, I bent then,' cherruped old Daniel. 'Bent indeed!' sez his old 'ooman. 'You bide quiet. Doctor knows best.'

H.J. Massingham
*A Countryman's Journal* (1939)

# Cider

Men can easily get drunk on cider; but they do not suffer for it next day, if they have pure cider of fermented apple-juice and nothing else. Unhappily, this wholesome drink has given way to other drinks that are less wholesome. A shrewd observer said to me: – 'When each man had three pints of cider every day, there was not half this bickering and quarrelling that goes on now.' And that, I think, is true. They were always in the genial stage of drunkenness, and seldom had the means of going beyond that. A few, however, very often went beyond; and they have been described to me as 'never proper drunk, nor proper sober neither, but always a-muddled and a-mazed.'

This failing was not confined to Devonshire. My father notes in his diary, 7 August 1847, at Dinan in Brittany: – 'The apples thick beyond conception, and the priests already praying to avert the evil consequences they apprehend from the plenty and cheapness of cider.' He writes to my grandmother from Dinan, 15 August 1847: – 'The apples are so abundant this year that the country will almost be drowned in cider. How they will consume it all is a wonder, for they export none. The lower orders are drunk, it seems, a great deal of their time. The priests always pray for a bad apple crop as the only hope of saving the people from perpetual drunkenness.'

A former rector of Lustleigh was remonstrating with a man one afternoon for reeling through the village very drunk. But the man had his reply: – 'Ay, 'tbe all very fine for you to talk, but you goes home to dinner late, and us doesn't see you after.'

Cecil Torr<br>
Small Talk at Wreyland (1979)

# Scrumpy

In the true country inn, a clubbable meeting-place, drunkenness is very rare, partly, no doubt, because the beer is so much lighter in content than in pre-war days. But that is not altogether the reason, for the home-made wines, a traditional Cotswold industry, are of fearful potency. One evening I set forth to the Baker's Arms to taste a 'rate' compounded of scrumpy (local cider) and beetroot wine. The brew is comely to look upon, being a ruddy colour like the robin's breast, but a tack so flaming that, though I drank but a pint, I felt I was crossing mid-Atlantic in Noah's Ark. Once in the open air, I drove straight into the ditch.

Yabberton is noted, not only for its 'yawnies' (simpletons) but its brews of home-made wines – cowslip wine, rhubarb wine, dandelion wine, coltsfoot wine, elderberry wine, blackcurrant wine, green gooseberrry wine, that tastes like champagne only better, parsnip wine, potato wine (the strongest in the world), plum jerkum (so called because it gives you a jerk), and tip wine, brewed from the fresh shoots of the bramble. One Sunday the parson preached against the inn and on the next against those private inns into which several houses in the village were converted. During the following week a bull of mighty girth and picaresque disposition pushed open the door of his pen, deposited the farm hand with one handsome toss into the pigsty and took the road of liberty and adventure. The reverend, who was importantly engaged in the churchyard, took him for a cow and said 'Shoo!' Rufus disregarding God's acre and the cloth, lowered his uncompromising head, thundered into the churchyard and made for the Established Church, which tumbled up a hayrick outside the opposite gate as though Satan and his legions had left the Underworld. There he abode for four hours, clamouring for Rufus to be shot. But Rufus had cost his goodman eighty pounds, and from a safe distance he assured his elevated pastor that he would soon go away. Yabberton vented a universal 'Sarve he right,' and has been convinced ever since that Rufus had been providentially chosen to defend its ancient rights ...

The local brews, though their survival is precarious, still keep their heads above fizzes, still differ from village to village, both in colour – usually paler than Woodpecker or Bulmer's – and flavour. And if the demand year by year declines, a few tales of the giants still survive. The other day a carter in my village consumed seventeen pints in three hours. At the close of the inundation he remarked, 'This be doen I no good. I'll try a pint of beer.' Then straight as a die, he walked home.

While I was sipping the deep-flavoured inspiration of scrumpy-cum-beetroot wine, there stepped into the half-timbered bar, with happy lights twinkling along the beams, the worthy, hatchet-faced but with the soft Cotswold hazel eyes, of whom is told this yarn. Once while he was driving a wagon up Weston Hill, the children home from school climbed into the back. Joe turned round and growled, 'Bloody well don't.' But when the children laughed at him and continued to shout and ride, he once more turned round, and in his hoarse, chanting voice called out, 'Then bloody well do.'

H.J. Massingham
*World Without End* (1932)

# 3 July 1791, Lincolnshire

Great-Hale Fen is now all enclosed, and flourishing with corn; and the roads over it are super-excellent, of a light loomy sand. Arrive at Swineshead, a small market town; here I made enquiries after the old abbey of Swineshead, (by all the names of enquiry) of a young man; to whom, at last, I said, 'Are there any ruins?' Who answer'd, 'I know of no breweings'. An old man did assist me: 'Why it is to the left, not a chain mile out of town'. So I found the scite thereof, and a good farmhouse upon it: where long did I call and halloo, as I saw a cap at a window, seemingly of a woman; at last out came an old fat farmer in his nt cap, who was very civil, begg'd me to alight, and drink rum and water, or what I chose; and explain'd to me where he believed the old priory stood. He then took me into his garden, and shew'd me where a famous yew tree grew, that was a sea mark; the stem of which was sold to a miller for £20, for a mill post. Mr Gough in his new edition of Camden, says that this tree now stands. Most authors write from hearsay, and from the books they consult over their fireside; but never move to an observation: now I examine the place with my own eyes. He shew'd me, likewise, the stone figure, fixed in the outside of the house wall, of a Knight Templar; of which he accused himself of having (when a boy) often shot at with a pistol, and then glorying at carrying off his nose: which he now thinks of repairing. 'When I buries my cattle', said he, 'that died of the distemper, I got into the burying ground of the monks, and dug up many of their skeletons.'

John Byng
*The Torrington Diaries* (1954)

# Christmas at a Village School

Thirty years spent working in an Infant School has provided moments of humour, at Christmas in particular:

'I think Father Krismus and Jesus are best friends.'

'The Holy Gost came to see Mary in a dream and the gost said to Mary you are going to have a little baby and Mary said oh gosh.'

'Baby Jesus was born with a round yellow hat an 3 Kings came to arsk Mary's hand in marage and they brout her lots of presents.'

'Everybody loves baby Jesus even my sisters and my brother but I don't. I love the 3 wizmen best becus they brought presens.'

Elsie Olivey

# Which Hole?

The farmer's wife bent down and whispered in my ear. I nodded and made for the well-worn path that skirted the privet hedge round the garden and led to a small brick shed. I was familiar with the brick shed now but the first time I had visited the farm's earth closet I had been perplexed at being confronted with three identical holes in the long wooden seat, each with its own wooden lid. I had worked out that as the farmer's family comprised father, mother and son the three holes must be a father hole, a mother hole and a son hole, and though I was shocked at the idea of their all using the lavatory together I realised how glad I should be of companionship if I'd had to go so far from the house on a dark winter's night. But the question was, which hole I should use? I imagined the family's grumbling, like the three bears, 'Who's been using my hole?' and so fearful was I of using the wrong one that I decided to risk having an accident on the way home. After all, I could always blame it on the pigs.

Lillian Beckwith
*About My Father's Business* (1971)

# Country Characters

# Work to Rule

Old Sam knocked at the side-door of the Post Office about 8.30 one morning and asked the postmaster if he would accept a telegram for dispatch when the office opened at nine. He had barely time for his five-mile walk over the moors to catch the bus to market, and the telegram was urgent. The postmaster was feeling irritable and refused, saying, somewhat obscurely, that it was 'idleness, sheer idleness' on Sam's part to make such a request. Sam didn't argue, put the telegram in his pocket and set off on his long walk. When he got to market, he sent off his belated telegram and then called on the newsagent, where he ordered a daily paper to be sent to him by post for six months. The postmaster was also the postman, and Sam's farm lay two miles off the road along a narrow lane and then a cart-track, stony in summer and deep in mud in winter. Every day the paper had to be delivered. Sometimes when Sam was taking his churns to the main road for the milk-lorry, he would meet the postman. The first time this happened the postman offered him the paper, but Sam wouldn't take it; he knew that by rule it had to be delivered at his house. As the postman trudged along the lane behind the milk-float, he heard old Sam muttering something that sounded like, 'It's nowt but idleness, sheer idleness.'

Dorothy Kahan
*The Countryman Anthology* (1962)

# Sam the Blacksmith

As regularly as Sam Turner the blacksmith received his Income Tax forms, he tore them up and threw the pieces on the forge fire. At last, even the postman became alarmed at such irresponsible defiance of the law. 'You'd better do something about it, Sam,' he would say, handing in yet another official buff envelope. 'Yes, midear,' came the quick reply: 'here's what Sam'll do about it' – and once more he tore the form into fragments and tossed them on the flames.

But one day, when he was sitting in the kitchen, eating his dinner, there came a knock at the front door. Mrs Turner went along the passage to see who it was. 'There's two gentlemen to see you,' she announced on her return. She was rather excited; but then anything out of the usual run of things is sufficient to excite Mrs Sam. 'Oh, is there?' was her husband's calm response. 'It's a long time since I saw one gentleman in these parts, let alone two. Let's have a look!' But first he emptied his plate of rice-pudding.

One of the visitors stood in the porch. He held a bundle of papers in his hand. The other stood out in the garden path, watching from a distance. Sam surveyed them both. Then the man in the porch informed him that he was an Income Tax inspector, and handed him a paper. Sam took it but did not even bother to examine it. Without a word, he pushed his bulky way past the inspector, tearing the form into shreds as he went. At the bottom of the garden he stopped and threw it into the stream.

'Do you know what you've done, Mr Turner?' asked the astonished official. 'Of course I do,' answered Sam, as he took up his stand again in the doorway. 'Of course I do. I've chucked that old bit o' paper in the stream. Didn't you see me? And if you want it back, I dare say you'll find it somewheres down past Linsell's shop by now, I shouldn't wonder!'

The inspector curbed his tongue. He smiled, knowingly. He had met old countrymen like Sam before. He thought he knew the way to handle them, 'Can I come inside for a moment?' he asked. 'Yes, you can,' answered Sam. Then he pointed to the inspector's mute companion, who was still standing watchfully in the pathway. 'But he can't,' he added. 'He ain't opened his lips all the time he's been here; and I on't have no dummies in my house. He can go and take a walk in the sunshine, or he can sit out there in the motor-car, or he can do whatever he's a mind to; but he on't come in my house – no, sir, he on't!'

Sam led the way into his front room. He offered the inspector a chair. Mrs Turner, meanwhile, had been anxiously listening out of the bedroom window. Now she came to the top of the stairs. Nervously she clasped and unclasped her hands. She wished Sam would be more careful, speak more respectfully. The inspector laid his hat and gloves on the table and glanced for a moment at the stuffed white owl staring from under its glass dome in the corner. Sam took his ledgers out of the bureau and handed them to his visitor.

Now it should be known that Sam 'does his books' every Sunday morning. It is a ritual, taking its accepted place in the morning's routine of rest. Did you ever see a facsimile of Dicken's signature, with all its embellishing loops and scrolls? Sam's handwriting is very much like that. It will therefore be readily understood that he takes a long time 'doing his books' on a Sunday morning. He may not be interrupted. Mrs Turner sees to that. It will also be understood, I am sure, that the results of all this labour, though lucid enough in their maker's eye, are calculated to bewilder anybody less familiar with the elaborate script.

'There you are, sir,' said Sam: 'now you can see for yourself.'

Exactly how much the inspector could see for himself, I would not like to guess; but for ten minutes by the sonorous clock on the mantelpiece, he scrutinised those florid pages. As patiently as he could, Sam endured the silence; but presently he could keep quiet no longer. 'Stands to reason,' he said, 'I ain't got anything left over, come the back-end of the year, to pay taxes on. There's my new anvil, there's my coal, there's –' But the inspector was not listening and so Sam left his many expenses untold. The clock continued to tick on in the silence. Mrs Turner tiptoed down the creaking steps. 'Yes, you can see for yourself,' Sam repeated, as if suggestion itself would make it so. 'It's all in there. What comes in and what goes out. And – well, it's as much as I can do to make 'em balance, let alone leave anything over.'

The inspector closed the ledgers and gave them back to their owner. He was a discreet man; and what his careful search had revealed – if anything – he did not say. Gravely he looked at Sam. 'You'll get yourself into a muddle, Mr Turner,' he said. 'Do, that on't be the first time,' was the surprising reply: 'I mostly as in a muddle, one way and another.' The inspector smiled. 'But see what a lot of trouble you could have spared us,' he said. He felt he was handling the situation very well. 'If you had filled in those forms we sent you, we shouldn't have had to come all the way out here to see you to-day.'

This was too much for Sam.

'And a nice ride you've had, too, ain't you?' he said. 'All in the sunshine! I tell you I ain't got time to be everlastin' writing letters and things: not like you, I ain't. Nobody pays me for writing letters, same as they do you.'

The inspector looked at his wrist-watch – as if the clock in the room had not been announcing every second as noisily as it could. He held out his hand. So far as he was concerned, the interview was over.

'Well, Mr Turner,' he said, 'I see that everything is in order. But will you do something for me? Will you just fill in this form, put it into an envelope, and post it to me as soon as possible?'

To his official, clerical mind, no doubt, it all seemed simple enough, reasonable enough. But Sam thought otherwise. Quite apart from his present mood of obstinacy, there was the fact that he shares in ample measure the general countryman's antipathy to forms of all kinds, and the more-than-antipathy to committing anything to paper. 'No, sir,' he said; 'that I on't!' And then, quickly ransacking his mind for some excuse, he added: 'for one thing, I ain't got any envelope.' But the inspector soon overcame this little difficulty. 'There,' he said, producing the necessary envelope, 'now will you do as I ask?' Sam searched his mind for some further obstacle, but his invention, that works slowly at any time, seemed now to have forsaken him altogether. 'Maybe I will, come Sunday,' he answered, accepting the hand proffered in farewell: 'I'll see.'

C. Henry Warren (1944)
*The Land is Yours*

# The Sexton

Tommy is a slight-built man, not very tall, grey-headed, and with a small straggling bit of beard. His face is wrinkled and weather-beaten, for his life has been spent wholly out of doors in the fields, and with the cattle. His voice is always very hoarse, and in addressing you he leans his head towards you, and speaks very loudly, in a raucous and almost uncanny tone. You can always tell when he is near by his loudly-uttered words, though no doubt he thinks he is speaking in a most subdued manner. His hair is rough and curly. On Sunday he wears a high linen collar, the corners of which stick out in something of the Gladstonian manner, and which gives him an old-time appearance. His coat is of the swallow-tail order, of black cloth, and trousers of the same. His small head is crowned with the bolero. In the winter afternoons and evenings he is to be seen with old-fashioned horn lantern in one hand, and a bundle of large keys in the other. He visits the church at all times of the day and night; he is not a bit nervous. Besides being sexton, he sees to the lighting of the lamps all round, and in the porches too, as well as to the fires for heating. Very often in bright moonlight nights these show conspicuously; but when it is pitch dark they are out. Everyone then passes humorous remarks about the lamps, and cries aloud for Tommy. It is either the wicks or the oil at fault, or the wind has blown them out, or something else, but there is no complaining.

Tommy is intensely proud of his graves, and regards them all with fatherly care and affection. Sometimes he is deputed to renovate a mound, and keep it in order permanently. Then, whenever you meet him, he is certain to be full of the matter, all he can talk about is the clipping and paring and tidying up of the turfs. Notwithstanding his great deafness, if you should happen to ask the old man if he would like a drop of whisky, though your voice be ever so moderate, he hears well enough then. 'Jest a leetle drap,' he says.

Tommy had to attend an inquest one day as witness, concerning an unfortunate son who died suddenly. Of course, he understood nothing at all, and could not be made to do so either. The coroner was furious; he was raging mad almost. Poor Tommy was an object of extreme pity. As soon as the coroner handed him the Testament to take the oath, he began rummaging forth the spectacles and opening the pages; he thought he had to read a chapter. Several times the coroner tried to make him understand; then the storm broke. He shouted, raved, roared, and bullied the old man most shamefully; he was livid with passion, but Tommy was unperturbed. He kept giving his unsolicited evidence with child-like simplicity. 'Listen to me!' the coroner shouted, with his mouth in the old man's ear. 'LISTEN TO ME! LIS-TEN TO ME!' You could hear him fifty yards away outside. Then, in a fit of desperation he concluded, 'Take him away! TAKE HIM AWAY! TAKE HIM AWAY!' So the old man was led outside, and the testy coroner proceeded with his business.

Alfred Williams
*A Wiltshire Village* (1912)

# Bruiser versus Doctor

The Four Shires Stone is an undistinguished monument which stands at the meeting-place of four county boundaries – those of Gloucestershire, Oxfordshire, Worcestershire, and Warwickshire. Upon it many undistinguished persons have carved their undistinguished names, and yet, perhaps because of the hardness of the stone and perhaps because of the purity of the Gloucestershire minds, there is not one scrap of pornography to be found on either of its four faces. The Musa Latrinae has left it alone.

This was the scene of my great-grandfather's exploit: and the story goes that he was driving his gig on his rounds towards Chipping Norton when he came upon a very large and angry crowd standing about the monument. In the middle of this crowd was a very large and angry prize-fighter; and when my great-grandfather got out to inquire what was the matter he was informed that – let us say – Bob Brown, the Bourton Basher, was billed to fight Willie Smith the Warwickshire Wizard at the Four Shires Stone upon that day, and here was Bob Brown, but Willie, thinking discretion to be the better part of valour, had failed to turn up. What was more, Bob was very angry, and the people were very angry, since many of them had walked twenty miles to see the fight, and Bob was raging and roaring that he'd take on any two of them for the same purse that had been offered to the craven Willie; but none of the crowd were disposed to accept this offer, for Bob looked very fierce indeed.

'Very well,' says my great-grandfather. 'I've a case of measles at Little Compton, and a smallpox at Adlestrop, and John Jones' wife confined with her tenth at Barton-on-the-Heath, but, damme, I can spare the time to give Bob Brown a hiding if he wants one.'

The crowd cheered, and the Bourton Basher roared: 'Bare fists?' and my grandfather nodded and told somebody to hold his horse. And then the people made a ring, and my great-grandfather quietly sailed in to Bob Brown and hammered him and hammered him until he'd had enough; and then my great-grandfather called for his horse, and wiped the sweat off his forehead and the blood off his broken knuckles, and quietly drove off to the measles at Little Compton and the smallpox at Adlestrop and his wife of John Jones confined with her tenth at Barton-on-the-Heath.

John Moore
*The Cotswolds* (1937)

# The Feud

The feud that broke out between Joe Partridge and Albert Jenkins last winter has just had a belated repercussion. Everybody had hoped that the matter was all settled by now, but apparently it has been smouldering in Albert's mind ever since. It was two years ago when he lent Joe Partridge some parts out of his mowing-machine; and yesterday morning when he heard that Joe had begun his hay-making he suddenly remembered the loan. Not having any grass to cut of his own, his machine stands dropping to bits in the shed, and he had forgotten all about the borrowed pieces. Rumour says that it was not a loan: 'Yes, take 'em,' he had said, when Joe asked for the parts, 'an' kip 'em.' But there was nothing in black and white to prove as much, so as soon as he heard Joe's machine working up at the Steading he hurried off to the police and asked them to help him get his mowing machine parts back again. The police complied and Albert marches off triumphantly with the driving-rod and several other odds and ends under his arm. And now Joe's machine is idle and the grass stands uncut. Furiously he mutters against Albert and wonders whether the blacksmith will be able to get the necessary parts made before the weather breaks.

C. Henry Warren
*A Cotswold Year* (1936)

# Widow Earry

I were down on the low marsh a-cleanin' o' the deek where it run in the river, an' I sees summat a bobbin' past an' catches hold on it. 'Pears to me, I says, that's the parsnip what near cost Widow Earry her life. How's that? Well, a week back, Widow Earry she got out at eleven o'clock time, an' get a skip o' parsnips out o' the hale at the foot o' the garden, an' off down to the river to clean 'em. The river, that ran full swab last week, an' that there natterin' ole wumman, what must she du but be so fumble-fisted she let one fall an' dop arter it, an' over she go – head fust inter the water that be runnin' a flood. An' she give a holler an' a shruck, till she git such a bellyful o' water she can't holler no more. Two chaps what were workin' nearby, they hears she an' come a-runnin' an', dang me, there she were a-floatin' along with all her skirts aspread a-holdin' of her up, an bobbin' as like as like could be to an ole dive-an'-dop. Then she spits out the mud an' begins to holler again fit to freeze yer blood. Them there chaps, they couldn't help but laugh, not but what the pore ole gal was in a bad way, an' they off with their coats an' pulls her out down by the bridge afor' she git in the pool. She were properly dozzled and dodderin', so they carries her home, an' the neighbours, they gits her into bed, an' what with hot bricks an' tea she were right as rain come evenin' time. Her son, he took on proper, he did, an' telled she she be a silly slummakin' ole mauver a-riskin' of her life over that there parsnip. Wimmen be dunt-headed enough, they can't think, pore things.

Lilias Rider Haggard
*The Countryman Anthology* (1962)

# Please, Sir, Please

The trap turned into the street drawn by Bandage the pony – so called because he had a broad band of white round his tummy like a frayed rag – and Father got in beside Uncle Dick. I climbed up behind them and tucked myself in to the deep straw that littered the floor. The strawed floor was not meant for my comfort but for bedding down the piglets which Uncle Dick expected to buy and with whom I should have to share the straw on the return journey. Sometimes if the pigs were noisy or restless my discomfort would be so great that I'd think to myself I wouldn't ask to be taken again, for no matter how uncomfortable I was I did not dare make a whimper of protest in case Uncle Dick heard. The big horse whip reared itself so menacingly within reach of his right hand that I had no doubt he would use it on me if I displeased him. I used to stare at his large unyielding back and think about the poor orphaned children who had once been taken in the trap for their first glimpse of the country. The orphans, three little boys, were protégés of some menial of the chapel on whom Aunty Rye wished to bestow a more magnanimous reward than her usual gift of a cold rice pudding so it was at her instigation they were commanded to take an afternoon's airing with Uncle Dick. Having been repeatedly enjoined that in return for such beneficence they must sit perfectly still throughout the whole journey and not utter a sound, the mouselike little boyos had burrowed into the straw hardly daring to lift a hand in response to the goodbye waves of their guardian. The silence had lasted until the trap had left the town and was proceeding along a deserted country lane when a small voice piped up tremulously, 'Oh, please, sir ...'

Without turning his head Uncle Dick had sternly rebuked him, 'Quiet there!' he commanded and drove on.

'But please, sir,' another voice piped up more urgently after they had travelled a while longer.

'Less noise from you children or you'll be put out of the trap and have to walk back,' rasped Uncle Dick again without turning his head. They had covered a good distance before a third voice was courageous enough to try and attract his attention.

'Please, Sir, please ...' The plea ended with a sob. Uncle Dick was outraged. It was bad enough having disobedient children in his trap – but blubbering children! He reined in Bandage and turned round ready to quell the three orphans with savage threats. But there were only two little figures in the straw and the door of the trap was swinging open. 'Please, sir,' they sobbed piteously, 'our Willy fell out a long way back.'

Uncle Dick had turned the trap and driven back immediately,

of course, but they had to go nearly two miles before they found
Willie lying in the road with both his legs broken.

Lillian Beckwith
*About My Father's Business* (1971)

# Henry Wheeler

[From conversation of G.E.L., 16 January 1894] 'You've heard
of my mother's cousin Harry Wheeler? No? Sure you must have
heard of him. I should think he was as strong a man as anybody
ever heard tell of. He took my uncle once – my Uncle Walter,
you know – and laid him on the table: and then, by a
handkerchief tied round him – round here you know (i.e., round
his middle) lifted him up with his teeth!' 'No! By George, did he
though!' 'Ah, he did! As nice a fellow as ever you need see; – a
nice good-hearted gentlemanly fellow – only he drank so you
know – well that was the cause of his death, poor fellow: but
except for that – ah, he was a capital fellow ... He come in once,
you know, and he says to my mother "Tilly," he says, "Tilly"
(that's her name you know) "Would you sooner be lousy, or have
a lousy look?" She see how it was with him, you know, so she
says, "Well, I don't know, Harry." "Don't ye?" he says, "well,
I'd sooner be lousy; 'cause you could get rid of 'em." I suppose
he thought you couldn't get rid of the look, if you'd got it. Hi hi
hi.

'He had a leather suit made once, for shooting you know. And
when he'd got this, he come into our place, – we were little kids
then – and he says: "Well I never. Did you ever, See a monkey
dressed in leather"; and I can remember how we laughed, – we
thought that was clever.

'He always used to rent the shooting down at the Pond. Well,
one time there was a party there, going coot shooting: he was
there – of course he would be, renting it. There were a couple of
men staying at the Pondhouse, – Londoners. Well, when they
heard of this shooting party, and found out who 'twas, farmers
and so on, you know, they rather pooh-poohed it – wanted to
make out they was a little better, I suppose. Well, these two, they
goes out with guns; – took couple of hundred cartridges, were

out all the afternoon, and came back with one coot they'd shot. At least, I daresay they shot it; though some of 'em about at the time said they'd found it. Well, when they came into the house, Harry Wheeler was there, in the barn you know, and he'd heard about these gents. So by and by they come in, and he asks 'em all about it. What they'd shot? How many cartridges they'd taken out and so on. And when he'd found out all the ins and outs of it – he was a bit gone, I suppose – he turns on 'em, and calls 'em – well, pretty near everything you could think of. Till at last, one of 'em couldn't stand it any longer, and he turned upon him, and answered him back again. But Harry, he looked at him, and he says, "Look 'ere! If you says that again, I'll hit you, just like that!" And he banged his fist clean through the panel of the door. The other chap turned white, and made his way off.

'He didn't mind what he did, when he was a little way on. But as good-natured, you know, – there, he'd give away anything. Father and Mother was up at his place once; and coming away, he took 'em into his greenhouse. "Here, Till," he says, "you must have this flower; aye, and this one, look, Tilly. And Willum, here: put this 'un up in the cart too." Well, he kept on, until they'd got the tail of the cart (little dog-cart, you know) piled up with flowers. So then his wife whispered to my father, "You ask him for one or two more." So Father says, "I should like to have this one too, Harry." "Well then you won't 'ave 'un: and you won't have no more at all: an' I goo' mind t' say as you shan't have them you got up in the cart." That stopped him, directly, you know, – being asked.

'But he would drink – that was the pity of it. His wife locked up the cellar, and took the key. Well, he went down with the powder flask, and blew the lock off the door. He would have the drink: and that's what killed him, poor fellow.'

George Sturt
*The Journals* (1941)

# At the Yew Tree Inn, Wye Valley

The background for these evenings was provided by the local worthies. Twice a week the grocer came in. He was rather pale of face and wore spectacles, and bringing out a notebook and a fountain pen from a waistcoat pocket, he would take the orders which would be delivered on his next visit. Thus he would go into conference over a pint of beer with Dora, who towered over him from the other side of the counter in her pink knitted shawl. The first time I saw him, he brought news of two lads who had escaped from Borstal and who were apparently running wild over the countryside. The details of their adventure which, I fancy, he exaggerated a little, kept on getting mixed up with the groceries. I only heard snatches of the conversation, which ran something like this:

'How are you for rice? The police tell me that these boys broke into a farm-house early to-day and stole some money from the farmer's wife. They were big, strong fellows. You haven't seen anybody suspicious in your bar this evening?'

'Now I come to think of it,' answered Dora, 'I served an ale to an entire stranger. He was young and strong. I don't know if you would call him burly.'

'You should be careful,' the grocer went on with a malicious twinkle. 'Two women alone in an inn ...'

'That was no Borstal boy!' put in Esther. 'He knew this part of the world.'

'All the same,' said Dora with rather less assurance, 'I don't like the idea. I'm going to run upstairs and see that all the doors and windows are closed.'

A few minutes later she came back, drawing her shawl tightly around her shoulders. 'Everything is quiet,' she announced with a slight tremor in her deep voice. 'Now let me see. We were talking about rice. How about some semolina?'

'Semolina?' answered the grocer. 'I haven't seen any for six months. But to return to these Borstal boys ...'

Mrs Robert Henrey
*Siege of London* (1946)

# Heard at an Inn

I had just come out of an inn where I had listened for nearly two hours to the rich, rough, wise talk of the men who live at the heart of England, compared with which the talk at a West-end dinner table is barren and sterile, and the conversation at a cocktail-party is like a chattering of idiots. I had come to the pub soon after six, having walked very leisurely up the north side of the ridge from Guildford – for on this last day of my holiday I was disposed to take things easily and to enjoy myself. In the bar, when I first entered it, were four old gnarled labourers talking about the affairs of a farm that had the delightful name of Christmaspie. They did not invite me to join in the conversation, nor would it have been much use if they had, for I did not know the cow called Blossom that was recovering from milk-fever, nor the field called Starveall where nothing would grow, nor the damp wood-corner in a neighbour's meadow where already in the early mornings you could find 'darzed great mushrooms as big as dinner-plates, so that they look like paper-bags left there arter a picnic.' It appeared that one of the old men on his way to work had taken the liberty of helping himself to some of these mushrooms, and, to his enormous indignation, had been reproved by a keeper. If the farmer himself had caught him, he would not have complained but a keeper! – 'I said to 'ee, I said, thee keeup thy pheasants and thy hares and thy coneys, but thee bain't keeuper of mushrooms, I said, thee doant go shooting mushrooms, do 'ee, so leave I alone and stick to thine own job!'

'Quite right,' agreed the other old men. Clearly the keeper had exceeded his duty. 'Mushrooms don't fly on wings nor run on legs neither.'

'I'd never,' said the landlord with a wink, 'have the impidence to ask a man for a stewing of mushrooms.'

'Thee'd take un without asking!' laughed the old men, who had heard the joke before.

Now there came into the bar a great glorious barrel of a man, with round red face and tun-belly, a hogshead on legs, who nevertheless had been working in the fields all day, for when the landlord asked him how he was, he said, 'I be fair forswunk!' using Chaucer's word as if it were common speech. The others, indeed, accepted it as such; and I felt a queer thrill of excitement at hearing a man use that verb 'swink' even as the Wife of Bath had used it in 1390. I sat in my corner and fairly hugged myself in secret joy and wonder at the continuity of English things.

But there was better to come; for when that great walking tub had swallowed its five pints and departed, swallowed them as if they were but teaspoonsful, the landlord winked at the old men, and the old men winked back, and one of them said:

'Old Willum 'd swap his wife for a barrel of beer!'

John Moore
*A Walk Through Surrey* (1939)

# Pork

He is simply a memory with a voice, both of them slightly aided by a present of whisky from an old employer, and in the sun of April he sprouts like any cottager's garden with alyssum and tulips.

Food is a great subject with him, and especially roast pork, from which it is perhaps fair to conclude that it was not often to be had. One bout of it he often recalls. He was still in his prime, a big man of fifty, and though he had been threshing all one morning – 'it is a good many ups and downs of the flail to a pound of pork' he says – he had eaten no food and he had none by him and there was none in the house. Presently hunger so far mastered him that he stopped work and took a walk round the farmyard. There he saw a fat pig lying on his side, heavy and making bacon rapidly. In a short time he had laid his plans: lifting up his flail he began to thresh the pig, and shouting above its screams: 'Son of a fool, I'll teach you to eat my dinner.' Nor did he cease to beat the pig and to upbraid it for stealing his dinner until the farmer came out and, pitying his case, sent him out a dish of roast pork to make amends. Then he tells a story to celebrate the incomparable joys of such a dish. An old woman had died and two young wives came to lay her out. After doing their work, they sat down on the bed, talking of many matters. Soon they fell to discussing pork. One said that it was best in the middle of the day; the other that it was best at night; and the debate was hot and threatened to be long, when the corpse rose straight up in the bed and said in a gentle voice that it was good at all times, then lay back in peace and never moved again.

Edward Thomas
*The Heart of England* (Dent, 1906)

# A Last Word

An old countryman who had always lived in the same parish, was approached by a newcomer. 'There's a funny lot of people living in this district,' said the newcomer.

'Ah,' replied the gnarled old countryman, 'an' 'tis a funny thing, they do keep on acomin' here.'

Anon.

# Index of Authors